Cottage Cheese Thighs

Jenn Sadai

Jan-Carol
Publishing, Inc
"every story needs a book"

Cottage Cheese Thighs
Jenn Sadai

Published May 2016
Express Editions
Imprint of Jan-Carol Publishing, Inc

ISBN: 978-1-939289-95-7
Library of Congress Control Number: 2016943167

You may contact the publisher:
Jan-Carol Publishing, Inc
PO Box 701
Johnson City, TN 37605
publisher@jancarolpublishing.com
jancarolpublishing.com

This story is dedicated to my handsome husband,
my gorgeous mom, my stunning friends and every woman or man
who has every struggled to love their reflection in the mirror.

Letter to the Reader

I know what it feels like to hate your body. I've cried over my reflection too many times to count. I'm tired of watching my self-esteem sink whenever the number on the scale starts to rise. I've spent the majority of my life battling my weight and it's time for me to win this war!

Developing a body that didn't make me cry was the intention behind writing this story, although it blossomed into something greater than I ever imagined. Instead of figuring out how to create and maintain a body that resembles the flawless images I so desperately wanted to imitate, I taught myself how to love my existing body, flaws and all.

This story dissects society's views on what constitutes a beautiful body, as well as the pressures women face to look and behave a certain way. Too much emphasis is placed on our appearance rather than our attitude, abilities and accomplishments. Investigating my insecurities gave me a chance to separate my self-esteem from the scale and realize my true value in this world. I've never felt more confident and capable. I pray it does the same for you.

Jenn Sadai

Foreword

By Ms. Camay

Cottage Cheese Thighs is a book every woman in the world should read. I've always been admired for my self-confidence and fearless sense of loving my full-figured body my entire life and have never been obsessed with the size pants I wear. I never fought a battle with any scale I met, however, reading this book created a sincere sense of compassion for other women. This book will expose the damage mainstream media is causing among women around the world today through the personal, intimate story the author courageously shares with you.

Her life-long journey to loving her body and her 'cottage cheese thighs' will force you to look at your body and any aspect you pick apart with a completely different mindset. Our bodies are a miracle, created to give life, live life and survive life. Our fingers feed us the food that nourishes our body. Our arms hug the people we love. Our stomach stretches and expands miraculously allowing human life to grow. Our legs carry us over many miles and yet, we allow our mind to overpower our opinion of ourselves and the strength of our physique. Although I don't share the same body confidence issues with this author, reading this book has empowered me to continue to be a piece of imagery in the world today that sends the message to other women that, "YOUR BODY IS BEAUTIFUL!"

Ms. Camay is a Humanitarian Award Recipient, International Best Selling Author, Radio Personality, National Lifetime Titleholder and Coach in Plus-Size Pageantry. Visit her online at www.mscamay.com.

Acknowledgements

My sincerest appreciation to Kim Harrison, Louise Smith and Jan-Carol Publishing, Inc. for lending your creativity and expertise to the book cover design. Special thanks to Rob Sadai, Christine Boakes, Rob Santarossa, Liz Cormier, Jeremy Boakes, Shawna Boakes, Rahel Levesque, Deb Birchard, Bill Birchard, Michelle White, Sarah Pinsonneault and Kim Chapieski for their constant support and encouragement. I'm truly grateful for everyone who supports my dream.

Every BODY is Beautiful

Being Confident is Brave

Over the last few years, there have been quite a few people—friends and strangers—who have referred to me as being brave. It caught me off guard in the beginning. Brave was not a characteristic that I would have ever used to describe myself prior to publishing my first confessional. I've always equated bravery with more life-endangering and heroic endeavors. I certainly haven't risked my life.

In all honesty, I actually interpreted the comment in a negative context. I thought my family and friends were calling me brave for publishing *Dark Confessions of an Extraordinary, Ordinary Woman* as a polite way of saying I'm crazy or intentionally setting myself up for emotional devastation. It felt like everyone else knew it was a bad idea that only I'd have the nerve to attempt.

I associated bravery with being crazy in regards to myself, because I couldn't fathom the idea that people truly thought *I* was brave. My inability to accept the compliment as being true meant I was still struggling with low self-esteem. Despite the fact that I was encouraging courageous confidence and self-acceptance on my social media platforms, my own self-worth was still fragile. I had the confidence to set tough goals and chase my dreams,

1

but I was constantly battling doubts and insecurities when it came to what others thought of my behavior and physical appearance.

Fortunately for me, I've figured out an effective technique for squashing my fears and proceeding in spite of it. When I catch negative self-talk sneaking into my head or slipping from my lips, I use the same logic and compassionate advice I give friends when they put themselves down or question their capabilities. I've always been a pretty good friend to everyone *except myself*. I've finally realized that I need to treat myself with the same love and concern I give to others.

Another way I push past my insecurities is forcing myself to take my own advice. I attempt to comfort and lift others up with inspirational posts on social media about loving and accepting yourself, flaws and all. I owe it to those who believe the things I share to actually live up to my confident image and practice what I preach.

Instead of thinking the term "brave" must be a cleverly disguised insult, I focused on justifying it as a legitimate description of myself. I've gained a lot of confidence over the last two years, and I can now see why some people might consider me as brave. I've trained myself to embrace it as the compliment it was intended to be. I haven't risked my life, but I've repeatedly put my reputation and talents on the line for the world to judge. I sacrificed my pride and privacy in an effort to encourage and enlighten others. That takes guts and I'm shocked with the details I've been willing to share.

People assume that someone who exposes her deepest confessions and dirtiest secrets to anyone willing to read them has to be either courageous or foolish. I definitely don't consider myself a fool, since my bravery wouldn't even exist if I wasn't willing to trust in my talents. I believed I was good enough to succeed as a writer before writing my first paragraph.

I recognized and accepted the personal risks I was taking when I published all of my past mistakes. I don't believe that being honest about my faults will have a negative impact on other people's opinion of me. Everyone has done something in their life they're not proud to admit.

More importantly, if it does change someone's view of me, it won't have any bearing on how I live my life. It only proves that person must not have known me very well in the first place. Although I hid my depression and abusive relationship when I was struggling through it, I've always over-shared my experiences when it came to my flaws and failures. At least, I usually do when it comes to people I trust.

I can rationalize why some might refer to me as brave if I talk myself through it. So, what makes a brave woman, who's willing to put countless mistakes from her past in writing, not courageous enough to wear shorts in public that expose her cottage cheese thighs?

Why does that same woman still refer to her thighs in such a deroga-tory way?

That one irrational insecurity can instantly shake my newfound self-esteem. I can't seem to comfort myself the same way I do when my char-acter or intelligence comes into question. On those rare occasions, when I've ventured outside the house in shorts that bare any part of my upper thighs, I'm ridiculously self-conscious the entire time I'm in public. I think everyone is staring at my legs in disgust.

In reality, no one else cares what my thighs look like or thinks it's inappropriate for me to be wearing shorts. I'm healthy and active. I know my legs don't look nearly as bad as I think they do. I realize how stupid it is for me to spend the entire time yanking on my shorts, so that they cover as much of me as possible...yet I still do it.

I have ample logic and compassion to talk myself out of this insecurity; however, I still haven't conquered it. I can't seem to convince myself that it's acceptable to expose my chubby white legs in public. That's why I now only buy shorts that go to the knee.

However, I'm just as embarrassed to confess that I'm so insecure over something so insignificant. I don't consider myself a vain person. I've never been overly concerned what people think of my appearance, except whether or not they thought I was fat.

My weight is the biggest factor in whether or not I feel attractive. I'm confident enough to appreciate and embrace my natural beauty. I wear very little makeup, rarely fuss over my hair, and normally choose clothes based on comfort and convenience rather than style. I'm sincerely happy being average-looking and refuse to waste a lot of time or money trying to make myself look any different than God intended, unless the occasion calls for it.

So why do I care that my thighs are a little dimply?

I finally think I'm ready to bravely flaunt every inch of my legs in a very public way. I plan on using this story to overcome my own insecurities, while helping others through theirs. I want to ensure that I've earned the high praise of being referred to as brave by the time I finish writing this book.

For me, titling a book based on a basically-true description of the back of my thighs is braver than admitting I've made some questionable decisions in my past. I'm telling the world that I've been hiding dimpled white skin behind my knee-length shorts and skirts. The unappealing nature of my upper legs is a part of me I've worked hard to hide, and now I'm choosing to draw attention to it. That will take guts and confidence.

I wasn't sure if my new story idea was feasible or necessary, so I decided to run the concept I was considering by some of the women in my life. As you will see throughout this story, I value the opinions of others, especially when I'm attempting to step out of my own comfort zone. Sometimes I ask out of insecurity; other times my questions are driven by curiosity. In this case, it was both.

I proudly announced my next book would fully expose my imperfect body in a way that would teach other women how to love their own physical flaws. I explained how I was going to achieve this massive undertaking, which would include chronicling all of my past and present issues with my body—giving honest accounts of my weight, my failed and successful diet attempts, and an in-depth look at why my self-esteem fluctuates with the number on the scales. Then I mentioned my idea for the book cover.

This time, no one politely told me I was brave. A few of my friends actually said I was crazy, especially when I described how I wanted the cover image to *highlight* my cellulite. One woman even said you couldn't pay her enough money to put her thighs on a book jacket, and she was relatively the same size as me, if not smaller. Maybe I *am* crazy!

If I use logic to overrule my initial, emotional response to my friends' reactions, it only proves this story's necessity. None of my friends would allow their own imperfect bodies to be immortalized in print, including my friends who had far better figures than I. Once I discovered how intensely every one of these women hated their own thighs (as well as the rest of their bodies), it became obvious that I needed to delve deeper into society's twisted image of what constitutes an attractive body.

The female body is beautiful, right?

There wasn't one woman I talked to who didn't list aspects of her body that she worked extra hard to cover up. The moms I know refuse to show off their stomachs because of their stretch marks. My friends who are past the age of thirty won't wear tank tops because of loose underarm skin. Every time I shared my intentions for this story with someone new, the response was loud and clear.

"My thighs are repulsive!"

"I hate my body, and I keep getting fatter."

"I wouldn't admit my real weight to anyone!"

"I've got more stretch marks and cellulite than skin."

"Only my husband sees me naked, and that's with the lights off."

Even two incredibly fit friends went on a rant about what they hated about their bodies and how they are obsessed with the scales. Regardless of their physical size, it seemed like most women shared the same insecurities that I feel. When I explained to these same women that my goal was to write an honest story journaling my battle with my own body-hatred that would encourage women (and men) to love their bodies at any size, the response was undisputable.

"Wow, I really need to read a book that will do that!"

Almost every woman had a story of how her imperfect figure had dis-suaded her from trying something, doing something or wearing something. None of these women were obese or even noticeably overweight, yet most of them admitted to being too insecure to do something they wanted to do because they were embarrassed by their body.

One perfectly healthy mother confided in me that she didn't join a baby and mom swim class because she didn't want to wear a bathing suit in front of the other moms. I didn't get to see the other moms in the class, but I guarantee they weren't all tanned, toned, and stretch mark free. I'm sure most of them felt just as self-conscious when they first entered the pool, but they figured out a way to get past their insecurities. They didn't let a little excess weight or stretch marks stop them from having a beautiful bonding experience with their child.

I see women heavier than me boldly wearing clothes I think I'm too big to wear—and they look absolutely fine. They appear to be confident and secure in themselves. I personally know several women who are great examples of confidently loving and accepting their bodies, even when they're carrying a few extra pounds.

Unfortunately, those women appear to be the minority. Even some of the most outgoing and physically beautiful women secretly harbor serious insecurities. They act like it doesn't bother them, but in most cases, it does. I guess I fit into that category. Up until very recently, I was hiding my hatred for my thighs because I didn't want to shatter the image of being a brave and confident woman.

I've been forcing myself to live up to the same leadership qualities I post on social media, because my books are based on being completely honest. That means learning to love these legs and being willing to flaunt them in public, even if they are not perfect. This story's purpose is to undo the last 36 years and train my mind into loving cellulite, fat cells, and droopy skin.

Shit, maybe I am crazy!

A book reprogramming our brains to love our physical flaws might not seem possible, but I'm up for the challenge. I recognize what goals I'll need to set for myself to be successful, and I'll need a general plan on how to achieve them. Once I figure out how I can love my excess fat, I should be able to teach others my technique.

My mission for this story is to dissect all of my self-esteem concerns, teach myself how to love my body—including my thighs—and make anyone who reads it feel better about their own body. It's won't be easy, considering I must first admit that I'm currently not as fit as I'd like to be. I'm writing this book at a time when I'm far from my ideal weight. I'm about twenty pounds heavier than my ideal size 6 body, and ten pounds heavier than what I would normally consider fit.

Lucky for me, I'm the perfect size to write this story. I'm right in the middle of my weight range. For this book to be effective, I need to learn how to happily accept my love handles, bouncy behind, and thunder thighs. I also need to stop giving random body parts horrible nicknames just because they don't embody the image I want to display.

I'm a human being, not an array of body parts.

My perceived image on social media creates the illusion that I'm in exceptional physical condition, but this body is far from perfect. My athletic interests and profile pics have given the impression that I've got the body every woman wants. I am regularly active and generally healthy, so it's not as if I'm pretending to be something I'm not. However, that doesn't mean I don't have a soft belly, excess skin sagging from the back of my upper arms, and what my ex used to call "cottage cheese thighs."

I used to cringe and then cry when I would hear that term being used. It would remind me of his cruelty, and re-ignite my intense hatred of my legs. I would envision the mushy cellulite that coated my upper legs and become obsessed with changing their appearance at all cost.

My thighs have never looked like any woman's I've ever seen inside a magazine. Well, unless it's one of those pathetic tabloids picking on some poor actress because she gained a few pounds. It makes me so angry when I see a close-up of some slightly chubby celebrity's legs at the beach playing with her kids and the caption reads: "She's let herself go" or "Worst beach body."

Seeing those magazine covers is one of the reasons why I hid my thighs for so long. I know that my ex's constant insults are partially responsible for my body image issues, but my insecurities started long before I met him. Prior to Shane giving me the title of this book as his favorite pet name, I used to say that my thighs resembled raw chicken skin because of their bright white and veiny appearance. That's not exactly a more flattering description. The sleazy magazines that prey on our insecurities and exploit our weight obsession are just as guilty as my abusive ex.

Those demeaning descriptions of my legs are somewhat accurate; however, they're highly exaggerated because I've been wearing "I hate my body" goggles for as long as I can remember. The only thing I see when

I look at my legs is that they're not the legs of a typical athlete or runner, which shouldn't really bother me as much as it currently does.

Despite the fact that I'm fearless enough to share all my personal drama and personality flaws with anyone willing to read them, I am not brave enough—at least at this point in the story—to share an actual image of my thighs with the world. I know the perfect image for the cover of this book would be a close-up of my dimpled thighs, but right now, I wouldn't have the courage to share that side of me with the world. Hopefully I can change my perspective, so I don't disappoint myself and others by chickening out.

Bye-Bye, Verbal Abuse!

The first plan of action is to stop insulting myself, and sadly, *that's not as easy as it should be*. I was raised by a mom who constantly put herself down, and consequently, I found myself tolerating several verbally abusive relationships throughout my life. I'm so used to being told everything that's wrong with me that I insult myself without even realizing it. I don't want to be that person anymore.

I escaped an abusive romantic relationship and overcame verbal abuse from a former manager. I owe it to myself to conquer the self-abuse I inflict every time my weight goes up or I try on a pair of pants that are too tight. I would never talk to my friends so cruelly if they gained a few pounds.

So why am I so hard on myself?

I know I'm not the only person to verbally attack their own appearance. In fact, it's rare to find someone who doesn't put themselves down in one way or another, especially women. Most complain about their bodies; however, their self-abuse can spread into all aspects of their lives.

"I'm such an idiot."

"I'm failing my kids."

"My house is a disaster."

Nothing we do ever seems like it's good enough, because it doesn't live up to the perfect images we see in magazines and on TV. We run ourselves ragged in circles trying to do too much, and then beat ourselves up if we fail to be a perfect spouse, parent, employee, and/or housekeeper.

The closest I've found to a woman who appears comfortable in her own skin and rarely insults herself would be one of my oldest friends. She recently lost a considerable amount of weight and is genuinely happy with her body. She worked hard for it, and looks absolutely amazing. It makes me smile to see her enjoying the initial rush of dropping several pant sizes and the pride that comes with such a major accomplishment.

I'm very familiar with that feeling. It's the "I'm happy with my weight because I know it could be worse" feeling, and it counteracts the instinct to dissect and demean your physical appearance when someone gives you a compliment. You want people to notice the weight loss and comment on your newly improved physique. That means being, or at least acting, happy with how your body looks.

To be fair, she was quite confident about her appearance before she lost the weight—well, as far as I could ever tell, at least. I know her mother instilled self-pride in all of her children. It is something I admire about their family. There have been phases throughout my life where I had the same level of confidence, but it was only when I was at the lower end of my turbulent weight range. My self-esteem has always been somewhat attached to the weekly results when I'd step on the scale.

Sadly for me, that feeling of self-assuredness has never lasted beyond the initial weight loss. I need to constantly maintain a strict level of fitness and diet to achieve the kind of results I want. What makes my effort even more pointless is that I think I am overweight unless I'm at my absolute fittest.

Maintaining a size 6 (which is the lowest I've ever made it) takes a huge commitment. Doing what's best for my body always needs to be at the forefront of my thought process for me to stay that size. That means analyzing everything I eat and working out daily. However, when I reached a point in my life where being fit became an obsession, I realized I wasn't tackling the *root* of the problem. My self-esteem was still tied to my weight, and I had to find the reason behind my obsession, if I was ever going to break the cycle of *self-abuse*.

Thinking about weight loss all the time isn't fun or healthy. There is so much more to life than your physical appearance, and I refuse to let it consume me any longer. Something inside me is convinced that I will figure out the reason(s) for my body image issues and use that insight to develop the same feeling of confidence, even when I'm carrying a few extra pounds.

I am writing this story to convince myself and others that my flawed thighs are perfectly acceptable. Our bodies don't have to be trimmed and toned to be considered healthy and attractive. More importantly, there's no reason for me to be ashamed of any part of my body. I'm not a fitness trainer, or a supermodel who gets paid to look a certain way. I have better things to do with my free time than chasing unattainable physical perfection.

Prior to publishing this book (I know I'm too stubborn *not* to put my thighs on the cover, now that I've put it in writing) there have been few people who have seen my bare thighs since I hit puberty. Besides a few months here and there, when I was in exceptionally good shape, I've always worn shorts or skirts that are long enough to cover the upper portion of my legs. I rarely swim in front of anyone except my husband, and I will wear shorts in the pool if there are other people around. I won't even bother trying on anything that doesn't look like it will loosely cover three-quarters of my thighs.

My thighs and rear end have always been the biggest source of my insecurities, although they were just the tip of the iceberg. When I was younger, I hated my frizzy hair and rarely wore it down. I used to also be self-conscious about my crooked tooth and would fight the crooked smile my mouth naturally forms (making it worse) any time someone took a picture of me. If my forced smile made me look awkward or unappealing, I would ask my family and friends to immediately delete the photo.

It's a sad way to live, and unfortunately it's quite common. I've listened to my stunning mother, gorgeous friends, and even my handsome husband critique photos of themselves. I'm not the only one who's asked someone to delete a photo from their camera or phone because we don't like the way we look.

"I look fat, please delete it."

"My hair's a mess, just delete it."

"It shows my double chin, delete it *now*."

"That's an awful picture of me; you better delete it."

I'm guessing that the majority of women and maybe half the men who read this book are guilty of asking other people to delete precious memories of us because we are unhappy with our appearance. I'm still guilty of doing it, if the picture is particularly bad, although I won't ask someone to delete it if the picture captures a special moment—even if it shows my double chin.

That's a brave step for me, but it shouldn't be.

No one is born with a heightened sense of self-consciousness, or this many foolish insecurities. We're all comfortable flaunting our plump bellies and pudgy thighs when we're crawling and giggling shirtless in diapers. You can't deny the cuteness factor of a chubby baby.

I can't recall caring about my physical flaws or my weight until I reached puberty. I started to gain weight when I was in grade seven, and I went from being a bony, 110-pound kid to a 130-pound teenager in only a matter of months. All of a sudden, none of my clothes fit me properly.

I lived with my mother at the time, and she never received child support from my father. They had a unique arrangement that put us at a financial disadvantage. My father covered my brother's expenses, and my mother covered mine. Although my mom made a good living as a bookkeeper for a large manufacturing facility, she couldn't replace my entire wardrobe one year before starting high school. The mandatory uniforms at the Catholic secondary school that I was planning on attending in a year were exceptionally pricey.

She bought me what she could afford from the discount racks, and offered me access to the few items in her closet that were big enough to fit me. Inopportunely, I suddenly weighed more than her—and have ever since, so my options from her wardrobe were quite limited.

Oddly enough, one of my favorite finds from my mother's wardrobe was matching raspberry polyester bell bottoms and a baby-doll maternity shirt that she wore when she was pregnant with my brother. It was the early

'90s, and retro hippie fashion was suddenly in style. My mom's maternity wear was certainly more flattering that the skin-tight clothes I was trying to squeeze into from my previous year's wardrobe.

Appearance is everything to a young teenager, especially for girls. In fact, it matters way more than it should to women of all ages. When your clothes don't fit properly, are not fashionable, or don't present you in the way you prefer to be perceived, it makes you feel like you're on display. You assume everyone else sees the flaws in your attire and are judging you for it.

Sometimes your suspicions are right and others are judging or mocking the way you look. Let's be honest with ourselves; every person reading this book has made a negative comment about someone else's appearance at least once, and it's almost a guarantee that a similar remark has been made about each one of us. It's the unfortunate state of modern society and something we need to conscientiously change.

I'm guilty of making fun of other people and I've been teased on more than one occasion, especially when I was young girl. It's a regular part of life for most teenagers, because everyone's trying to fit in. Their fragile egos cause them to believe if they draw attention to someone else's differ- ence, they will distract their peers from seeing their own. Fortunately, most people grow out of it. Sadly, some people take longer than others and a few never do.

The first time I can recall being made fun of was about my clothes, and it happened really early on in grade school. It was back when I was still a bony stick figure and didn't have any significant self-esteem issues. I'm guessing I was only in grade two or three. Despite how young I was at the time, I still remember the incident clearly because the incessant teasing stuck with me.

My grandmother had purchased a bright pink fur coat for me. I like bright, bold things, but this puffy, neon jacket was too fancy for my taste. I've always been more of a tomboy than a princess. However, my mother insisted that I wear it and I agreed, because it was a gift from my loving grandma. The first and only time I wore it to school, a couple of older girls followed me around, relentlessly picking on my vividly eye-catching coat, until I finally ran home crying.

"Is that skunk or pig's fur?"

"You look like a big pink hairball."

"Did you get your coat from a hooker?"

I specifically remember the hooker comment, because I had to ask someone else what it meant. I was too young to understand the meaning of their taunting, but old enough for it to sting. I refused to wear the coat to school again, and was thrilled when it was accidentally destroyed in the wash.

Fast forward a few years to the onset of puberty, and it only got worse. I was thirteen, switching to a new school and eager to make new friends. I was a little bit chubby for the first time in my life and forced to wear unflattering clothes that didn't fit right. Plus, I had the hormonal tornado of emotions that comes along with being a preteen.

It was bad combination, and resulted in an insecure young girl who could easily be coerced by peer pressure, and instantly devastated by the slightest teasing. I wanted to fit in at my new school, so I told lies to make myself sound cooler and used pity or naïveté to fend off bullying. It was the birth of my people-pleasing nature, and the slow death of my confidence.

My weight slowly increased even higher as I approached my first year of high school. I was never heavy enough for it to be a real concern, but I was always slightly larger than the majority of my female friends. They were still very lean, with only skin and muscles on their bones. I weighed around 140 pounds, had thicker thighs and a more developed chest. There was one close friend who in hindsight was slightly bigger, but I saw myself as being the heavier of the two. I always thought of myself as the fat girl in our group.

I'm not the only girl (woman) who sees herself as being larger than life. My mother is a perfect example of someone who thinks she is considerably bigger than her tiny frame and toned physique. She has always been in great shape, never overweight in any sense of the word, and undeniably beautiful from her head down to her toes. That's what the rest of the world sees, but not her. I've heard my mother refer to herself as being fat or insisting she needed to lose weight time and time again. The reflection she sees in the mirror is somehow distorted. It's an unhealthy trait I've certainly inherited, and one I'm now desperately trying to break.

Being tough on yourself, especially when it comes to your physical appearance, is not something unique to my mom and me. Many people experience the same optical delusion when they look at themselves in the mirror. In their mind, their flaws are all amplified and far worse than reality. In most cases, we bring it on ourselves.

Why do so many women inspect their faces within inches of the mirror?

Does anyone else actually get that close to your face?

Not unless you're passionately kissing someone—and then they're not normally thinking about your facial pores or bushy eyebrows. If someone is scrutinizing your appearance that closely during a romantic encounter, they can't be that into you, and are not worth your time in the long run. It's too hard to have a healthy relationship if you're with someone who's that concerned with the way you look.

I rarely look at my face that closely and when I do, I'm usually shocked. I prefer the illusion that I don't have wrinkles, uneven skin or the occasional gray hair. I don't notice it on anyone else, and I can't see it on my own face unless I stick a mirror within a few inches of it. Unless I've got a chin hair to pluck or pimple to pop, there's no need to get so close to the mirror.

Why would I torture myself by inspecting my face that closely?

I know I don't have the complexion I had ten years ago, and I can handle that. Eventually everyone ages. I hate to break the hearts of every young person reading this story, but wrinkles happen; you will get gray hair and saggy skin. Looks don't last, and that's why any healthy, long-term relationship has to contain far more than just physical attraction. That includes the relationship you have with yourself. Face it folks, all superficial beauty is temporary.

Our appearance is only a small portion of what makes up our essence on the earth. It's the pretty package that we use to display our compassion, capabilities, talents, and personality. I get that concept now, except when it comes to my weight. In my mind, I know my body size should be the most insignificant of all my attributes, yet it's the one that seems to control my self-esteem.

This book is my promise to myself that my confidence will now be based on my impact on the world, rather than my reflection in a mirror. As you're about to read, my weight has fluctuated drastically throughout most of my life. As a result, my confidence rose and fell with the number on the scale. I now realize that my confidence needs to come from something more substantial, like the person I've become, so that it doesn't drop the moment I gain a few pounds. I've still got a long and exciting life to live, and that scale will rise and fall many more times before I'm done.

Growing Waistline, Shrinking Confidence

Before I could attempt to retrain my brain into loving my body, I needed to pinpoint the outcome I expected and the path it would take to get there. Although most of the crazy goals I've achieved appeared to be spontaneous decisions, there was always a plan I had worked out in my head to figure out what it would take to accomplish such a feat. For example, before I ever breathed a word about this book to anyone, I pre-determined how much research, personal changes and commitment it would require.

I knew I wanted to be a more confident person, but I didn't want to change too much about my personality. I'm happy with my helpful and humble nature. I'm currently pretty content with my confidence level, except that I can feel it drop every time the number on the scale starts to rise. My intent is to separate my self-esteem from the scales and stabilize my self-confidence *based on the person I am.*

There are basically three levels of self-confidence. The basement, low self-esteem, is where your ego is fragile: you feel insecure and inferior to others. People who lack confidence are usually extra helpful, work really hard, and care *too much* about their appearance. They desperately need to seek accolades and praise, because they are convinced that everyone else is smarter, better looking, and more capable. That's the person I used to be, and I am desperately trying to change.

The central level of the self-esteem scale would be confidence. This is where you realize that you are just as a smart, good-looking, and talented as everyone else. You know you're valuable to the world, and that opinion of yourself is not easily shaken. Real confidence comes from loving all aspects of your being.

The over-the-top level of being confident is arrogance. That's where you think you are more intelligent, attractive, and gifted than everyone else. There are people throughout the world who see themselves as being more desirable than their true physical appearance. It amazes me because I've battled with the "I hate my body" or "I'm not good enough" feeling for most of my life.

However, I've known people whose extreme level of self-confidence actually makes them less attractive. Take the classic narcissist, for example. They view themselves as being superior physically and mentally. I have no interest in reaching their level of perceived self-importance, but I do want to find a balance, where I feel like I am just as beautiful as everyone else.

At the time I wrote this book, I was significantly more confident than I had ever been in my life. I knew I was a good-enough person, and was proud of the life I had created. Unfortunately, history has taught me that my self-esteem can drop again without warning.

I was a bold and fearless kid in grade school, but certainly didn't feel confident when I entered high school. I had passed the 140-pound mark on the scales, and was inching my way towards 150 pounds. All of my existing clothes were uncomfortable and unflattering. My mom spent a substantial amount of money on the school uniform, so she could only afford a few new items for my social wardrobe. I felt like the chubby, unattractive girl who needed to be overly nice to fit in.

Maybe that's why I never really put much effort into my appearance? As long as I can remember, I've been a minimalist in regards to makeup, jewelry, hairstyles, and clothing. My mom was in her twenties during the 1980s, so she loved the big hairdos, full makeup, and dramatic, stylish clothing from that era. I saw all the work she put into her appearance and never felt like it was worth all of the trouble.

In hindsight, that was only part of my logic. I figured high school would be easier if I blended in. I didn't want to draw any unnecessary attention to myself, because I didn't think the boys would be attracted to me—regardless of how I dressed. There were obviously better looking (skinnier) girls in the school, and my hormonal classmates weren't discreet at hiding their interest. The boys picked on the girls they didn't find attractive just as loudly as they gushed over the ones they desired.

I'd rather be invisible than the *butt* of their jokes. I mean literally, since "Baby Got Back" was a hit song that year, and my backside was my most noticeable *asset*. Sorry, I couldn't resist the puns. I'd rather laugh than cry… 'cause "I like big butts and I cannot lie!"

I laugh at that song now, but there are a lot of songs on the radio that objectify women and break them down into body parts. Even more shocking is that some of these demeaning songs are sung by women! I love the Black Eyed Peas, but I can't listen too closely to the lyrics to "My Humps" or I'll realize just how incredibly degrading they are to women. There are a few more songs by Beyoncé, Destiny's Child, and Britney Spears that imply women are nothing more than sexy toys for boys to enjoy.

It's not limited to hip hop either; that's just my personal preference in music. There's a new country singer called RaeLynn with a song out titled "God Made Girls;" a friend recently sent me the lyrics and it made my stomach turn. I have no interest in ever hearing the actual song. It basically says God made girls so that boys will behave. How did we go from empowering songs like Lesley Gore's hit "You Don't Own Me" and Nancy Sinatra's classic "These Boots Are Made for Walking" in the 1960s, to songs that imply our purpose on earth is to complete a man?

Women were not put on this earth to satisfy the needs of men. That mentality may be a part of our current culture, but it's time for us to change the way we think. Women have their own needs, wants, and desires. I pray this book helps to empower women, and teaches them to make their own goals and happiness a priority. Women must realize their value as human beings has nothing to do with their physical appearance or ability to care for a man.

Women are often their own worst enemies. We compete when we should be collaborating. Instead of loving our own flaws, we point out each other's. Criticizing other people's physical imperfections serves no worthwhile purpose. It's more rewarding to appreciate the fact that we're each a one-of-a-kind work of art.

I don't worry about being teased over my weight at this age, but I definitely tried to avoid it when I was fourteen. I hated changing my clothes in front of other girls and rarely wore anything tight-fitting. The one friend I had at the time, who was probably a few pounds heavier, ended up making my lack of self-confidence even worse—well, at least until I realized that she was just as insecure as I was.

The school uniform sizes ran horrifically small, especially the unbelievably poufy light gray and yellow kilts. I was normally wearing a women's size 8, sometimes a 10. The uniform kilt that fit me was a size 14. I tried to squeeze into the 12, but the button looked seconds away from bursting.

The numbers that I felt represented my level of attractiveness kept going up, and my confidence plummeted as a result. When I confided my embarrassing kilt size with my close friend, her response wasn't exactly comforting.

"Yeah, they do run small. I had to get a size 12."

Her response confirmed my worst fear. I was now certain that I was the biggest girl in my circle of friends. Most of the girls my age were complaining they had to buy a size 10 or 12. No one else admitted to wearing a size 14, so I didn't share my number with anyone other than my most trusted girlfriend. Instead, I dealt with it by going on crash diets that led to binge eating, followed by purging, and the occasional secret power workout in my basement.

I would starve myself until dinner was ready, eat whatever my mom made, then throw up, and work out in the basement until I was soaked in sweat. It is a miracle I didn't physically make myself ill. That's probably partially because I wasn't very committed to my unhealthy weight-loss plan. I only did it for a few weeks, and didn't throw up all of my meals. Sticking your fingers down your throat is an unpleasant experience, to say the least. Plus, I knew the risks and physical damage it can cause, if you do it on a regular basis, and I didn't want my mom to catch on.

I'm pretty sure this is around the same time I first tried the ridiculous Saran-Wrap trick. I would wind plastic wrap tightly around my thighs and stomach, turn the hot water on full blast, and work out in my bathroom with the door closed. I thought I could instantly melt away all the excess fat on my thighs. Unfortunately, I could only last in the heat for about ten minutes, which isn't much of a workout and not an effective weight-loss strategy. It is, however, a great way to waste a lot of hot water!

It's not overly embarrassing to admit I tried this foolish gimmick a few times in high school, since teenage girls are known to do crazy things to look good or fit in. However, I remember doing this when I was with my ex in my early twenties—and even a couple of times when I was in my late twenties, and married to my wonderful husband. Fortunately, I'm finally wise enough not to buy into stupid lose-weight-quick schemes.

When I first took dieting to extremes, it was because I desperately did not want to be the biggest girl in our group. I later found out that I wasn't the only one who had to buy a skirt that was bigger than a size 12. The friend I mentioned earlier left her kilt on the floor of her bedroom and I took a peek at the tag. On some level, I must have known that she wasn't smaller than me. My suspicions were correct. She was wearing a size 16. I never called her out on the lie, but found comfort in knowing she had the same insecurities as I did. I couldn't hold it against her, because I was the same way.

It reassured me I wasn't the biggest, which ended my already-failing binge and purge plan. I still did random diets and sporadic power workouts whenever my clothes felt tight. I was pretty good at fighting my insecurities back then, because I saw the effects it had on my mom. She spent a lot of time on her looks; she was and is undeniably beautiful, yet she still verbally insulted her appearance on a regular basis. My mom has always been shy and insecure, so I always strived to be confident and outgoing. I guess I can thank my rebellious teenage ways for any confidence I did have back then.

I was so confident prior to dating my ex, Shane, that I had the guts to get up in front of my high school, lip-synching and dancing provocatively to "I Need a Man" by Annie Lennox for drama class. I was comfortable getting on stage where there was a good chance I'd make a fool of myself. Most people enjoyed my out-of-character performance, but as always, there were a few who made rude remarks. I remember the comments bothering me a little, but it didn't stop me from doing similar things whenever the opportunity arose.

I wasn't happy with my body at that time, but it didn't prevent me from being social and even daring. I did, however assume that my extra weight was the reason I was rarely asked out. In grades nine and ten, most of the guys in my school hadn't hit puberty. They were still skin and bones, which meant I weighed more than the majority. Most boys that young will only hit on girls that are skinnier than they are, due to their own feelings of inadequacy. It was easy to come to the conclusion that the extra pounds I was carrying were what made me less attractive.

Although I felt and acted confident in myself back then, there was definitely some serious self-doubt issues toying with my decision-making process. I was instantly attracted to any guy who showed any interest in me. I was so desperate to be asked out that I can't remember turning down anyone, at least initially.

I was thrilled when I landed my first serious boyfriend in the last year of high school. He was a little chubby in the belly and had stocky legs, so I didn't feel self-conscious when I was around him. I was so happy that someone was genuinely attracted to me that I couldn't see all of the reasons why I actually deserved someone better.

I was just normal-teenage-girl insecure when I got my first serious boyfriend: the ex from my first book, *Dark Confessions of an Extraordinary, Ordinary Woman*. I knew I was a little bigger than most girls my age, but I was still relatively confident in my personality, intelligence, and overall appearance. It was only the weight that really bothered me, and I hid my disappointment in my body well.

Unfortunately, by the time the relationship was over, my self-esteem issues had escalated to the extent that I felt all aspects of my being were inferior. My confidence began its slow downward slide when my ex-boy-friend would pinch my belly or upper arms. In the first year, he never really said anything critical about it. He would just silently squeeze my excess fat between his fingers when we were cuddling on the couch.

I weighed somewhere between 140 and 150 pounds, so I wasn't even overweight. That's my ideal weight now, and I haven't exactly grown any taller since high school. I just wasn't lean or bony like most teenage girls. I probably gained between five and ten pounds in the first few months we were together—typical relationship comfort pounds. I guess Shane noticed the extra weight, because he started commenting on my healthy appetite or lack of exercise. For example, he didn't think I should be able to consume the same amount of food as he did.

"You're getting a burger *and* poutine?"

"Holy shit, that's a huge plate of food!"

"You're really going to eat all of that?"

I ignored him in the beginning, because I thought he was just playfully teasing me. He wasn't in perfect shape either, and noticeably weighed more than I did. I didn't start cutting back on my portion size until after I saw the number on the scale pass 160 pounds. I made sure to always leave a little on my plate, so he didn't think I was making a pig out of myself. I would also try to eat healthier in front of him and save the more sinful food choices for when I was alone.

That may have been the beginning of my secret food habit. I have a horrible habit of binge eating when I'm alone. I still do it, to this day. I sometimes want my husband to go to bed before me, so I can munch on dinner leftovers, chips, or a chocolate bar without feeling guilty. My husband doesn't judge what I eat or comment on it, but I'm still working on undoing all of the damage my ex did to my self-esteem.

Later on in my life, I discovered doing the opposite of spending time alone was an effective weight-loss method. I would limit my alone time whenever I was trying to lose weight. I'd keep myself extra busy, making tons of social commitments, and would make sure to go to bed at the same time as my husband. I didn't binge when people were watching, so I made sure people were watching as often as possible.

Isn't it crazy, the mind games we play with ourselves?

Although I had a few issues with my weight and appearance prior to dating Shane, I wasn't obsessed with how much I weighed or constantly dieting. In the beginning of our relationship, I actually felt an increase in confidence because a good-looking guy was interested in me. I decided I must be more desirable than I originally thought.

My confidence dwindled as our relationship became more serious. What appeared to be innocent, playful pokes at my excess fat or healthy appetite quickly turned into his genuine disapproval of my less-than-fit figure. His subtle criticisms mixed with unconvincing compliments made me second-guess all aspects of my appearance. That's probably the real reason why I made Shane wait a year to have sex.

I've always said the reason for prolonging sex was my fear of getting pregnant, since I saw how hard it was for my mom to be a young mother. She was still a teenager, and had to put her own dreams on hold to take care of us. That influenced my decision to delay sex as long as possible, and made an excellent excuse whenever the subject came up.

However, the self-absorbed and self-conscious part of me was more concerned with Shane's reaction to seeing my bare legs. It used to disgust me when I would look at my thighs squished together on the toilet seat or crammed into a bathtub. Not only was there not a gap between any portion of my upper legs, they were melded together in an overflowing blob. There was always at least one bright red pimple, and it seemed impossible to keep them perfectly shaved.

I was convinced that Shane would dump me the moment he saw my thighs. I was brutally rejected in grade eight because the guy I kissed said I had a mustache. The first guy who dumped me in grade nine said I gave him the confidence to finally ask out the girl he always liked. The second guy I dated in grade nine never gave me a reason; all of a sudden it was obvious he was avoiding me.

That was my pathetic track record with boys before Shane, and I didn't want to repeat it. I was falling hard for him, and thought it was real love. I didn't want my bright white, pimply, dimply legs ruining it for me. Even when I finally caved and had sex with him, I made sure the lights were off before revealing my inner thighs.

I was always too worried about my body to enjoy sex with Shane.

For those who've read *Dark Confessions of an Extraordinary, Ordinary Woman*, I won't rehash the horrid details of my toxic relationship with Shane. Let's just say it went from love to loathing gradually over the course of six years. He would pick on all aspects of my self-worth, insulting everything from my intelligence to my social skills, and most frequently, my body.

I was able to stay relatively fit for first year of our relationship, but ended up packing on another ten pounds by the time I finished college. I suddenly weighed over 170 pounds and didn't see any hope of losing them. I didn't care what I weighed, because I was slowly giving up on life.

I was living with Shane and trying to soothe my relationship struggles with Saltine crackers and processed cheese slices. I was also smoking a lot of marijuana, which almost always resulted in either eating an entire bag of chips or splurging on Chinese takeout. Sometimes it would be a massive bowl of popcorn, if I was broke or pretending to be dieting. I would eat until I felt stuffed, then smoke a joint so I didn't feel as full, and then eat something else to fill the void again. It was shameful cycle and I knew it, which only made me eat more.

The bigger I got, the more I hated my body, and the less I wanted to do things in public. I spent most weekends watching TV, talking on the phone with friends, and pigging out while Shane was having fun at the bars. Obviously, that behavior only added to my weight problem, literally speaking. By the time our dysfunctional relationship ended, I was only a few pounds shy of weighing 200 pounds.

I hated all aspects of my being.

Although weight was not the only reason for my self-hatred, it did amplify all the other flaws I saw in myself. I didn't feel attractive or worthy of a good life, which made me feel like my only choice was to stay in a very toxic relationship. I didn't think anyone else would ever love my flabby body. When our relationship finally ended (at his suggestion), I was tempted to reconcile every time I saw him. I was lonely, still having sex with him, and convinced he was my only option.

Waist Shrinks, Confidence Slowly Expands

After my awful relationship finally ended, when I was at the highest weight of my life, a twisted miracle happened. I lost over fifty pounds in only six weeks, without really trying. I wasn't eating or sleeping properly. I was living with my father, and avoiding the house as much as possible. I was under obvious stress from ending a lengthy, abusive relationship. Most people, including myself, assumed the weight loss was the result of a dramatic change in lifestyle.

I didn't care what the reason might have been; I was thrilled. I was living every overweight person's dream: losing weight without effort. The best part was being able to rub it in my ex's face. He made the mistake of asking me why I couldn't have lost the weight while we were still together. That was the last time he saw me naked!

I finally had a body that I was proud to show off, and I made sure that I did to everyone except Shane! I bought tighter and more revealing clothing. I even danced in a tiny dress on stage at a strip club, which was completely out of character and incredibly fun. When I went on my first trip to Las Vegas a few months later, I was so obsessed with showing off my new physique that I ended up asking a stranger to take a photo of me in my bikini by the hotel pool. I wanted undeniable evidence that I was no longer fat.

Unfortunately, my sudden weight loss was actually due to hyperthyroidism and I was seriously sick. This is going to sound perverse to anyone who doesn't already know my quirky way of viewing the world, but the illness was a necessary part of my recovery from the verbal abuse.

It was all part of God's plan.

My ex had crushed my confidence. He convinced me that I was ugly and unlovable. Prior to the thyroid issues, I thought no man would ever want me until I lost the weight. I didn't have the willpower or determination at that time in my life to lose the weight on my own. I needed a miracle, and received one by the grace of God.

For anyone who takes their religious beliefs quite seriously, please don't misinterpret my use of the word miracle. I'm not saying God miraculously granted me a better body because I was deserving of it. That would be a far-fetched and egotistical assumption, especially to someone who just admitted that she once enjoying dancing on a stage at a strip club.

I only mean that God knew I needed a confidence boost to get through a very difficult time, and allowed me to get sick so that I had enough self-esteem to save myself. My new trimmer physique was attracting positive attention from men almost immediately and that, in turn, began to rebuild what Shane destroyed.

Let me be very clear: A woman should never base her self-worth on the reaction she gets from men. It's very difficult for the person I am now to admit that a serious illness and flirtatious men were the real catalysts that cured me, after years of insults and criticism from an abusive man.

Men have nothing to do with my current confidence. I'm more annoyed than I am flattered by it now, especially if it comes from strangers or friends of my husband. Guys can adore me if they truly know me, but shallow compliments based on my appearance have no bearing on my self-esteem. My current obsession with my thighs has nothing to do with impressing men. I care more about what the women who read my stories and believe in my mission think than any man.

At that time in my life, I was insanely insecure. The life I was trying to hold together for the past six years had fallen apart beyond repair and I thought my life was no longer worth living. I needed reassurance from others, especially men, to overrule all of the demeaning and degrading things my ex-boyfriend had said to me over the past few years. Losing that weight gave me the confidence to put myself out there, which attracted some positive attention while distracting me from my broken heart.

I honestly doubt I would have been strong enough to survive the breakup if I hadn't lost the weight. I barely survived that time in my life, even with my slightly elevated self-esteem. I came frighteningly close to ruining my miraculous slimdown by ignoring the other signs and not seeking medical attention for several months. My eyes were bulging out of my head, my heart would race erratically, and my hair was noticeably falling out. My mom finally forced me to see a doctor, who immediately sent me to a specialist. I was prescribed thyroid medication to slow down my metabolism.

I must confess that I had no intention of taking the pills when I was first diagnosed. I didn't want to get healthy, because I associated health with a bigger body. In the beginning, I would only take them if my heart was racing, or I saw a clump of hair in the tub after a shower. I was afraid that if my thyroid was normal, I'd gain all of the weight back. Being thin made me feel like I was desirable for the first time in years, and I didn't want to lose that feeling.

This was obviously a low point in my life.

Hating your body so much that you ignore serious health concerns just to stay thin is a sickness in itself. I wasn't taking the thyroid medication as frequently as it was prescribed, and I experienced several frightening heart-racing incidents after my diagnosis. I drove myself to the hospital twice because I feared the worst. I waited in the parking lot until my heartbeat slowed back down.

I was desperately trying to overcome depression from leaving my ex, and working hard to regain confidence in myself. I'd battled my weight most of my life, and I didn't feel strong enough to either prevent myself from gaining weight naturally, or still love my body if I did put some of the weight back on. Hyperthyroidism gave me a necessary break from being overly self-conscious about my body.

Doing what was best for my well-being became a delicate balancing act. I needed to feel good about my body, while still caring enough about my health to take pills that had the potential to make me gain the weight back. Every woman who has ever struggled with her weight understands exactly how difficult it is to do something that may cause weight gain.

Fortunately, other aspects of my life started getting better. I was working a lot of hours and finally making a dent in the debt I'd accumulated with my ex. I met some genuinely sweet gentlemen, my current husband in particular, who seemed to appreciate more than just my looks. I was successfully pursuing my dream business with one of my best friends, and I was determined to turn my life around.

However, I was still experiencing many of the same symptoms I had before my doctor determined it was hyperthyroidism, and I finally realized that I had no other option than to take the problem seriously, even if it meant gaining weight. I started taking my medication regularly, attended all doctor's appointments, and made a remarkably fast recovery.

I only gained a couple pounds when I first conquered my thyroid issues. I stayed in the low 140s for the next two years, before slowly putting almost all of the weight back on. Yes, I went from weighing almost 200 pounds, down to under 140 pounds and then back up to over 190 pounds.

Regrettably, my new weight issues could also be linked to my love life. I wasn't overeating eating because I was depressed. I was now overeating because I was in a healthy and loving relationship. One of the genuinely good guys who had been giving me some positive attention at my part-time job quickly turned into my lover, and then my boyfriend.

No, that is not a typo or editing error. I was insecure in my body, still plagued by trust issues from my ex, and struggling to allow any men to get physically close to me. William soon became the exception to the rule, but I desperately fought the urge to become emotionally attached to him.

I had only had sex with one man other than my ex-boyfriend. It was a short-lived relationship that started about a month after I finally cut ties with Shane. I felt obligated to have sex with him after a few weeks of dating.

I didn't have any feelings for him, didn't feel particularly attracted to him, and we only had sex a few times over the course of our three-month relationship. I finally ended the relationship by placing a breakup letter in his mailbox. Without a doubt, he was the rebound guy.

My relationship with William, on the other hand, started as a wild, drunken and extremely passionate night unlike anything I had experienced before. He was older and appreciative of my young physique, so I didn't feel self-conscious around him. One night led to another, and there was just something about him I couldn't resist. I knew I was too messed up mentally from my ex and the rebound guy to get into another serious relationship, so I told him that all I wanted was a purely physical relationship. There are very few men in this world (if any) that would turn down an offer like that from a much younger woman.

I promised my loving husband that I wouldn't share any details of our love life out of respect for his children, so let's just say his ability to care for both my physical and emotional needs is the reason I ended up marrying a much older man. He let the relationship move at my pace, and encouraged me to be completely, unabashedly myself.

It took me years to truly trust William, but he never actually gave me a reason not to trust him. I was pretty fragile and insecure when we met, and he gave me distance whenever I asked for it. I'd run out on him in the middle of the night, and he would just patiently wait days or weeks until I missed him enough to come back. After about a year of a very untraditional relationship, we officially became a couple.

I was expecting the stress and emotional rollercoaster that accompanied my first long-term relationship, but we never really had any of that drama. We'd have the occasional insignificant fight, but we got along and genuinely enjoyed each other's company. We could cuddle on a couch, eat, drink, and be merry for hours upon hours, day after day.

We were usually either watching television or playing board games with his children, but that always involved snacking on pizza, fried foods, ice cream, chips, and other calorie-packed temptations that I wasn't used to being around. Since leaving my ex, I became accustomed to cooking only for myself. I could live off salads, soups, and stir-fry, which were healthy for the most part. Now, our busy schedules and full house often resulted in processed, packaged dinners or takeout food.

Although I wasn't eating or exercising the way that I should to stay healthy, I was happy with our life together. William was constantly complimenting my figure and reassuring me that he loved the way I looked regardless of any weight I gained. His kind words contradicted every awful thing my ex said about me. I think that's why I was able to watch the scales rise without freaking out over it.

When we married two years later, I weighed about 155 pounds. I was still happy with my body, and didn't stress over how my body looked in my wedding dress. Of course I still hated my thighs, but even they still looked a lot smaller than they did before the hyperthyroidism. I was healthy, and honestly felt beautiful on our wedding day.

Scale Goes Up,
Confidence Goes Down

It didn't take long for me to realize that I couldn't remain a fit body without putting any effort into it. I gained fifteen pounds over the next two years without realizing it. I gradually put on another fifteen pounds the following year. I was becoming settled and sedentary. I rarely stepped on a scale and only noticed the extra weight when I had my annual doctor's appointment or needed to buy new clothes.

Gaining a little weight wasn't the end of the world to me because I had a good job, secure relationship, and happy home life. My husband showed no signs of disinterest over my weight gain, so I didn't pay much attention to it.

However, it wasn't just my body that was starting to get too comfortable. My work wardrobe was a reflection of just how relaxed I had become. I went from wearing classy fitted suits and daring heels to black dress pants, knitted sweaters, and comfy flats. I've always been a bit lazy with my appearance, but it became a ritual to dress casually, apply a smudge of eyeliner and pull my hair back into a loose ponytail. I was a hard-working, easy-going employee who didn't want to be judged for how she looked.

That was my initial mindset, but my stance weakened every time I went up a size. Eventually, maybe inevitably, my security in my relationship with

William no longer felt quite as secure. The heavier I got, the more I felt the need to go above and beyond for him and his children. I didn't feel like my body was earning my place in his home, so I insisted on being the perfect housewife and stepmother.

I need to explore this mindset, since it's directly related to my confidence level and the very reason I decided to write this story. Up until recently, I never felt like being me was good enough for anyone to love. I was a people pleaser who thought I had to go the extra mile to get others to like me. This is a common trait, especially in females, and it adds unnecessary stress and anxiety to everyday tasks.

Despite the fact that I had a full-time job and paid half the bills, I still felt this compulsion to manage all "womanly" aspects of our household on my own. I'd get home from work at 5:30 p.m. and immediately start cooking dinner. I'd serve it, clear the table, and wash the dishes afterwards. I spent several nights a week washing and folding laundry, and another four to five hours on Sunday cleaning the house from top to bottom. I ran the errands, kept track of our appointments, and drove his children whenever they needed to be.

I have a strong feeling most women reading this book, especially those over the age of thirty, are nodding along with my description of daily life. I've noticed the younger generation is cluing in that household responsibilities should be a joint effort, but in most cases, the woman still manages the majority. Don't get me wrong, there are many men who are willing to do more...if asked. However, most men are smart enough not to volunteer for thankless chores.

The problem is women are less likely to ask for help, and seemed compelled to volunteer when others are in need. We feel like we have to prove ourselves, so we end up doing more than our share. I've seen this with my mother, my friends, and even other women in the workplace. We have this overwhelming urge to care for everyone else before ourselves.

While writing this story, a very close friend of mine lost her grandmother. She was an incredibly sweet woman whom I had met on several different occasions, and despite the fact that she was far from being young, her passing was a shock to everyone. She was 85 years old, and still doing everything she could for everyone else. While waiting to paying my respects and give her family my condolences, I heard the same remarks over and over again.

"She'd never say no to anyone who asked for her help."

"She was his rock, and did everything for him."

"She volunteered for everything."

My friend later shared the heartbreaking news that her grandma was tracking her symptoms and had been aware for a few weeks that something was wrong with her health. Unfortunately, she was so busy being everything to everyone else that she neglected to put herself first. That's an ailment many women suffer from without ever realizing it. My friend's grandma lived a long, wonderful life, and her kind nature wasn't the real reason she passed on. It's just an example of how so many women put everyone else's needs ahead of their own.

The same week my friend lost her grandmother, my husband and I came down with a nasty flu bug. I had it first, and it lasted about five days. I still got out of bed every morning, tried to work, did some writing, a little cleaning, and even cooking. William cooked me two meals, did dishes, and ran an errand for me; however, I insisted on doing a lot of things for myself. I had to force myself to rest every few hours and go to bed earlier than usual.

When William caught the same bug, he hibernated in our bed for three days. I served him everything he needed, and checked in on him every few hours to see if there was anything else I could get him (I felt guilty for passing my germs onto him). William had no problem resting the entire time he felt sick; as a result, he had a shorter recovery time.

By the third day, I started making him fend for himself out of bitterness. I knew it wasn't fair that he had the luxury of lying in bed all weekend, without a care in the world. Although William was helpful when I was sick, I still did most things for myself, including keeping up on laundry. I even washed all of our bedding to get rid of some of the germs.

Maybe my chores could have waited? Maybe William would have instinctually started serving me if I hadn't come out of our room for days? He's protective and pretty helpful, so it's quite logical this would have happened. I don't know if I could have properly rested when I was sick, because I rarely ask for help when I need it.

I'm getting better at taking care of myself and have finally learned how to leave work when I'm sick. I recognize that sometimes the best thing for me is to lie on the couch or take a nap during the day. I'm still not capable of putting my health ahead of everything else, but I've taught myself that sometimes a timeout from daily responsibilities is the most productive thing I can do.

So many women don't properly care for their own physical and emotional well-being, yet they'll go above and beyond to care of those they love. I'm not sure if this is true because it's our natural instinct to nurture others, or because it's our need to be needed. Some women might over give because of the insecurity that we won't be loved if we don't earn our keep. I know when I was at my heaviest weight, I believed the latter was the most dominant factor behind my people-pleasing behavior.

When I was unhappy with my body, I used to think that taking care of all household duties was a requirement of being a wife and stepmom. I actually believed that I needed to do an exceptional job of it, so William wouldn't fall out of love with me.

My older husband was obviously attracted to my young and firm 140-pound body when we first met. I had gained over 40 pounds, and my body was no longer a noteworthy selling feature. Wow, it's scary how easy it is to equate myself to a piece of property. I thought it was necessary for me to cook every meal, keep the house spotless without his assistance, and help care for his kids, so that he would stay with me.

I was completely disregarding the real reasons why my husband chooses to love me. I'm an intelligent conversationalist. I have a kind heart and a quirky sense of humor. We have fun together, and we enjoy each other's company. William didn't marry me for my fit physique. He loves the person that I am. Unfortunately, I didn't see it that way because I was struggling to love myself.

My self-esteem in social situations became embarrassingly weak, and I couldn't hide my jealousy. If we were in the company of a single woman with a better figure than mine, I'd automatically assume he was checking her out and wishing my body still looked like that. I was secretly wishing it did, so it only made sense that he would have the same train of thought.

I never caught him ogling or flirting with another woman. He has always been a friendly guy in general, and I never used to interpret his chatting with a beautiful woman as genuine interest until I started to gain weight. He has never given me any reason to doubt him, but when I was at my heaviest point in our relationship, I became convinced that he must at least wish he was with someone else. I've heard him make insensitive or rude comments about other women who were on the heavier side, so he couldn't possibly still find me attractive.

After one stupid argument when I know I was behaving like an insecure schoolgirl, I knew that I had to snap out of it before my jealous behavior ruined my relationship. I had to face the weight gain and figure a way to take back control of it.

The first step was stepping on the scale.

I'd stopped weighing myself several months prior, when it read 182 pounds. I was praying that it had gone down a little, and was dreading the possibility of shattering that illusion. I knew the majority of my size-12 pants were now too tight and I was mostly wearing size-14 clothing. I had a feeling the number was going to be a devastating shock.

I held my breath when I stepped on the scale, and exhaled tears when I saw the needle stop on 193 pounds. Once again, I was dangerously close to weighing 200 pounds. I was only a few pounds shy of where I was at before I lost the weight due to hyperthyroidism.

I was furious with myself. I understand how twisted this sounds, but I felt like my sickness was a gift: a chance for a fresh start as far as my weight was concerned. I was mad at myself for ruining my new body. As self-absorbed as this may sound, the moment I realized that I put all of the excess fat back on again, I felt like my world had just ended.

For those of you who've never been overweight, I would like to give you an idea of what it feels like to assess your entire worth from a number on the scale. Or at least this is how *I* felt, any time my weight was going in an upward direction. For anyone reading this who has felt the same way, I hope this reminds you that you're not alone.

At the times I was at my heaviest, I thought about my weight at least ten times a day—probably more. Every trip I made to the bathroom would end with me inhaling, holding it in, exhaling, and pushing my gut out as far as it could go while standing sideways in front of the mirror. I was testing to see what I looked like at my best and worst.

I'd evaluate how far my belly stuck out, compared with my breasts. I would check out how my ass and thighs looked, which have always stood out the most in a mirror. I was obsessed with my appearance, but not in the sense that I was putting any effort into it. In fact, my style of dress, my confidence and my activity level were directly linked to my weight.

When I weighed more than 170 pounds, I wore dark colors, big sweaters, and men's jeans because they were baggier in the butt and thighs. On the other hand, I wore bright colors, fitted shirts, and women's jeans when my weight was closer to 140 pounds than it was to 200 pounds.

Getting dressed and trying on clothes can be very traumatic when you're not happy with your weight. The worst blow would always strike you in a public dressing room, when you suddenly discover that the size you were wearing no longer fits. I've literally cried uncontrollably inside dressing rooms, because I was trying to squeeze into pants that wouldn't make it up past my knees. I'm willing to bet money I'm not the only one.

Seriously people, there are more important tragedies to cry over!

Every decision regarding my outfits, meals, and social activities was affected by my weight. As I put on the extra pounds, I started staying home more often on the weekends and would make excuses for avoiding large gatherings. I began to feel more insecure in my abilities at work, as well.

I tried dieting and pathetic excuses for workouts at home, but I never followed through long enough to see real results. I would lose a couple pounds, stop putting in the effort, and gain them back in less time than it took to lose them. My half-assed attempts to get in shape weren't working, and it was starting to take a toll on my self-esteem.

For those who've read *Dirty Secrets of the World's Worst Employee*, it was also a very difficult time in my professional career. All the confidence I built in myself since leaving my abusive ex was quickly vanishing due to an abusive manager. She was attacking my personality and capabilities at a time when I was verbally abusing my physical appearance. It was a lethal cocktail of abuse that could have easily pushed me right back to the depression I'd experienced six years prior.

I knew I had to do something, but after failing so many times, I didn't know what would work. The first time I dropped the extra weight, I shed the fat because of the hyperthyroidism. I had a horrible track record of failed diets, binge eating, and laziness. I had never obtained a fit figure the healthy way.

I was already considering taking up running and had recently started walking 10 kilometers (6.2 miles) once a week with some women from my work. One of those friends had shown me her marathon medal a few months earlier, and her sense of pride inspired me. She put the idea in my head that I could run one as well, and the more I thought about it, the more determined I was to do it. It seemed like a completely crazy dream, but I was searching for a challenge that would force me to get back into shape.

The first goal I set for myself was to quit smoking and finish a half-marathon.

In order to make this attempt different than all my prior efforts to improving my health, I decided to post my intentions publicly. At this point in the story, I cared way too much about what other people thought of me. If my status on Facebook said I was going to quit smoking and finish a half-marathon, then I felt obligated to do it. I didn't want to look like a fool or a failure in front of my Facebook friends. Yes, I realize how silly I sound.

Thankfully, my bizarre plan worked. I quit smoking cigarettes on my thirtieth birthday and finished my first half-marathon four months later. I was determined to reinvent myself as an advocate for a healthier lifestyle. I even joined a women's floor hockey league, and attempted belly-dancing (unsuccessfully). The encouragement I received from family and friends on social media was a huge help, and as a result, it inspired me to do even more.

Once I discovered that I was capable of defying the odds and able to tackle two challenging goals, I felt like I could do anything. I wanted to take it to the next level and transform my body into that of an actual athlete. I was a stoner in high school who smoked and drank too much to play sports. I wanted to prove to myself and others that I could be a confident example of physical fitness.

I sincerely enjoyed playing floor hockey and my weekly two-hour walk along the waterfront with my coworkers, but it wasn't enough. I wanted to ensure I had the physical endurance to participate in any similar opportunities, like a soccer league or aerobic dance classes. I was driven by the positive social interactions, rush of endorphins, and sense of accomplishment that came with being a part of the local fitness community.

Although I was physically healthier than I had been in years, I hadn't really lost that much weight. At that time, I probably weighed around 180 pounds, which was still far from the perfect body I desired. I didn't think I had a figure I could be proud to show off, because it didn't mimic those I saw on magazine covers or fitness commercials.

I still felt fat.

I will never forget my "no more excuses" moment. I was getting ready to go on a girls' road trip with a friend, my sister-in-law, and her best friend. We would be vacationing at a hotel with a massive indoor water park, which meant exposing my chubby butt and cottage cheese thighs in a bathing suit. I was so excited about the trip—until I tried on my suit.

I stood in front of the mirror and looked closely at my forward reflection. My thighs looked huge, but the rest of my body appeared just a little bigger than average. Then I turned around. It was the first time inspecting my backside in a mirror since I'd gained the weight back.

I was mortified by my reflection.

There were so many dimples, divots, and fat deposits scattered across my ass and legs that I was disgusted with myself. It was the worst my legs had ever looked, if only because I was too scared to look at them when I weighed closer to 200 pounds.

Once again, I burst into tears at the sight of my reflection. I couldn't hide my disappointment and embarrassment when William turned the corner to our bedroom and saw me standing in front of the mirror. He didn't look disgusted—he probably already knew how my thighs looked—but he did look sympathetic. He hates to see me cry.

"I'm going to change this, William. I'm sick of the way my body looks, and I want to get in better shape. I'm tired of hating my body," I rambled as I choked back tears. He stood there nodding supportively.

"Whatever makes you happy. You know I love you," he whispered gently.

"I'm doing it. You're going to see. I'm going to have real runner's legs. I will get rid of these cottage cheese thighs."

Referring to my legs the same way my ex used to brought back all the feelings of worthlessness I had during the last few years with him. The difference this time was that I knew I had a worthwhile life. I had the opportunity to live a happy life, and I refused to waste it being insecure and unhealthy.

A spark went off inside me, and I felt confident I would follow through this time. I said my intentions out loud to the love of my life, and was committed to proving myself right. I decided that this vacation would be the last one I spent wearing shorts over my bathing suit.

I ate and drank whatever I wanted during our mid-week girls' getaway, but made a point of squeezing in some exercise in the morning, when it was still too early to bring out the booze. I was silently, mentally prepping myself to tackle my weight as soon as I got home. I needed a huge physical challenge, one that was big enough to force me into becoming really fit.

My next goal was to sculpt a body that didn't make me cry.

I was watching *Biggest Loser* contestants finish a full marathon and decided, *if they can do it, so can I!* I loved the rush I felt when I finished the half-marathon. I was finally ready to fully embrace my goal, so I immediately posted on Facebook that I was going to finish a full marathon. I couldn't think of a more effective way to improve the appearance of my legs and strengthen my athletic abilities than training for a marathon.

Most people were quick to cheer on my new goal, although a few were concerned that I might be overextending my capabilities. I was still overweight, and had struggled to finish the half-marathon only a few months prior. A full marathon was a massive goal for anyone, especially for someone who had only been running (OK, slowly jogging) for less than a year.

I knew I had to get involved in something more physically challenging, if I was going to turn my body into a worthy example of physical fitness. Fortunately for me, my mom and stepfather own an insane kettlebell gym that specializes in high intensity, thirty-minute boot camps. I could tell just by looking at both of them that their workout classes were effective, so I finally forced myself to give it a shot.

My first attempt at the workout was horrifically embarrassing, or at least that's how it felt. I struggled to perform most of the exercises, and couldn't even squat without losing my balance. The workout consisted of two to three minutes of exercise, followed by a thirty to sixty-second rest. I was able to perform the moves for thirty to sixty seconds, and then I needed to rest for two to three minutes.

There were mirrors surrounding me, so I got to watch my thick thighs and bouncy butt as I failed miserably. I was especially mortified because my obviously older mom was not only able to complete the workout with ease, she was also a trainer. I assumed her clients must have been wondering how this super-fit, fifty-year-old woman had such an out-of-shape daughter.

I went to a friend's house afterwards, and started to cry when I explained how poorly I did. This friend was also overweight, probably more so than me, and had no interest in achieving a more active lifestyle. In fact, she encouraged me to give up on my goals.

"I just felt so fat and uncoordinated working out next to all those women with their perfect bodies."

"No point wasting time with skinny bitches who just make you feel fat. I wouldn't go back!"

This is about the same time I discovered there are two types of friends. There are those who inspire you to do better with your life, and those who try to hold you back. People who actively try to lift others up are sincerely happy with their own life and want to see everyone else happy. They truly care about their friends and value the relationships in their life. Those are the kind you treasure.

Friends who discourage you or put others down are normally not happy with their own lives. They don't want to see others succeed, because they don't believe they can achieve the same. As the saying goes, misery loves company—and the more miserable someone is, the less they want to be around happy people.

These so-called friends are concerned that if you gain confidence and feel better about yourself, you'll finally realize that life is more enjoyable when you're surrounded by genuinely happy and supportive people. That's why abusers attack their victims' self-esteem. They're afraid if they feel better about themselves, they'll realize they deserve better.

That particular friend is no longer in my life, because she made several unacceptable remarks about my supportive friends and tried to steer me away from my goals. I would invite her on walks, ask her to work out with me, and try to encourage her to make similar changes for her own happiness. Not only did she not want to participate, she actively tried to talk me out of my new devotion to healthy living.

I had (have) other true friends who wanted to go for walks and work out with me. They cheered me on and helped me get where I am today. I needed mutually-supportive relationships to be successful, and made several changes in regards to the influences I had in my life. It was necessary to lean on encouragers during the time I was training, because my confidence was still delicate and I knew mental strength would be essential to my success.

Feeling Fit and Fabulous

I was obsessed with becoming super-fit when I was training for my first full marathon. I knew I wouldn't be able to run as fast as the lifelong runners, but I wanted to at least have the same physique. I mapped out the level of commitment I would need for the next six months, the amount of exercise that would be required each week, the diet I expected myself to maintain, and how much progress I predicted I would see along the way.

I ran three or four days a week, went to my mom's kettlebell gym at least twice a week, and walked for two hours with my friends every Monday night. Some days I would run a few miles at the track, do a thirty-minute kettlebell boot camp and then go for an hour-long walk. My dedication was indisputable.

Anyone who has ever exercised this much knows the natural high it gives you. That rush of endorphins that provides you with endless energy and a permanent smile. I was hooked on it, and motivated to keep pushing myself. The further I ran, the further I wanted to run.

It was the same way with my diet. Every menu choice was based on how hard I would need to work out to burn it off. If I was at a restaurant, I ordered my food without condiments or cheese, always veggie or mushroom burgers minus the bun, and salad instead of fries if there was a side. That's when I switched to black coffee and started drinking more water. I did everything I could to reduce my bad calorie intake.

My conscientious effort to eat better and work out more frequently slowly paid off. It took me three months to lose the first ten pounds, and then I lost another ten pounds during the last three months of training for my first full marathon.

The loosely-structured training plan I created meant I was running thirty to forty kilometers a week. Running that often is a highly effective method of burning calories, which meant I could relax more when it came to my eating habits. I love food and it was hard to stay within a strict diet, so I allowed myself a treat once or twice a week.

A marathon is 42 kilometers (26.1 miles, for my American friends) and my longest training run ended up being only about 31 kilometers (19 miles). That run felt great—but two weeks later, when I attempted what should have been my longest run, I fell short of my goal. I was aiming for 36 kilometers (22 miles), and only made it 18 kilometers (11 miles)! It started raining, I had a headache, and my calves cramped up. I felt defeated and decided to turn around after only making it nine kilometers from my home.

I was in a lot of physical pain and absolutely terrified after that run. I thought it was a pretty strong indicator of how I would do during the actual marathon. I was disappointed in myself for only making it half the distance I planned. I gave up on my goal due to outside influences; that wasn't a reassuring sign, considering I was only a few weeks away from attempting a distance that could only be classified as crazy. Luckily for me, I felt it was too late to back out of my commitment.

I remember exactly how nervous I felt when I approached the starting line early in the morning on October 17th, 2010. I was grateful it was still fairly dark outside, because I was trembling and choking back tears. I was about to attempt 42 kilometers (26.1 miles), and the furthest I'd made it to date was only 75 percent of that distance. I was praying I had the mental strength to push myself at all costs. However, I still didn't know if my body had it in me. I knew how exhausted and sore I was after finishing

31 kilometers (19 miles). I was fighting doubt every step I took towards the starting line.

That moment in time will be etched in my brain forever.

I had three friends close by, but we weren't talking or even looking at each other. They were mentally preparing to walk a half-marathon. I was psyching myself up to something only one percent of the world has ever done. The loudspeakers were playing "I've Got a Feeling" by the Black Eyed Peas, and I had an overwhelming feeling that I was about to accomplish something that would change my life forever.

If you've ever run or witnessed the Detroit International Marathon, it's an amazing rush of excitement from start to finish. There are tens of thousands of people crowded together, all fighting their internal fears and anticipation. Everyone hops up and down to stay warm as they inch closer to the starting line. The course is scenic, challenging, and lined with complete strangers cheering you on. The finish line is boisterous and infectious, which is why most people commit themselves to participating in the event year after year.

The motivational atmosphere, the other runners, and my own stubborn willpower carried me to the finish line. I was able to run the first half without too much struggle, but my legs started cramping up around 26 kilometers (16 miles). I switched to a power walk and refused to acknowledge the pain in my legs and feet.

I wanted desperately to stop when I reached the Belle Isle Bridge, about 32 kilometers (20 miles) into the marathon, but received an encouraging text from the very friend who originally inspired me to run it. She was tracking my progress online and wanted to let me know how proud she was of me. That was the boost I needed to keep going.

I felt confident I wouldn't quit, even if it took me all day to finish. I started chatting with another woman, who was about my age and pace. She helped distract me from my body's utter exhaustion. Our walk was pretty slow by the time we approached the last kilometer, but we agreed that we needed to finish strong.

We started running as soon as we turned the final corner. Less than twenty steps into my final run, I felt a sharp, raw pain in the bottom of my foot – found out later I split the skin under my big toe wide open. I halted, coming to almost a complete stop—and then I heard my new companion yell.

"Don't stop. You said you wanted to finish strong, and you're almost there."

Her words propelled me back into a run, and I finished my first marathon in six hours and three minutes. That's almost twice as long as most runners take, but I'm still super proud of myself. My goal was to prove that I could overcome my doubts and push past physical pain to accomplish something challenging and fulfilling. I did exactly that, which inspired me to keep increasing the difficulty level of my physical capabilities.

It wasn't just the physical aspect of the journey that I overcame that day. I spent 80 percent of the distance completely on my own. Yes, there were strangers cheering, but I was left alone with my thoughts for over five hours. The old me couldn't have handled that much alone time.

Eight years prior, shortly after leaving my abusive ex-boyfriend, a close friend pointed out something I hadn't realized about myself. It was after about six months of being single, and we were talking on the phone while I was smoking on my father's front porch. This friend has always been brutally honest with me, and that day was no exception.

"You can't even go for a cigarette without talking on the phone. You can't deal with being alone."

Although I argued with her at the time, she was absolutely right. I didn't like the thoughts that crept into my head when I was by myself. I would always call a friend if there wasn't a TV or radio on to distract me from my own thoughts. I was unhappy with my life back then, and didn't want to face it. Fortunately, that was no longer the case during the race.

I loved the thoughts that crept into my head when I was running the marathon. I felt strong and proud of what I was doing. Even when I wanted to give up, I had faith in myself that I would continue and finish strong. I was sincerely happy with my life, and there was no room for any negative thoughts in my head.

It didn't even bother me when I crossed the finish line and discovered my friends were not there to congratulate me. The three friends I trained with were walking the half-marathon, and were supposed to wait by the finish line until I completed the full. I sent two texts to them before approaching the end and then another one after I crossed. There was no response and no sign of them anywhere. The woman I met near the end had already taken off to be with her loved ones, so I was alone at the finish line.

If this sounds depressing, it honestly was not. Not having someone there didn't take anything away from my feeling of accomplishment. It actually gave me a new sense of self-confidence. Nothing could wipe the smile off my face. I trusted my friends and knew there was a good reason for their absence (which there was, one friend passed out and was rushed to the hospital—thankfully she was fine). I just finished a full marathon on my own. I was comfortable enough with myself to celebrate the success on my own, as well.

Between 2010 and 2013, I wore a size 6, pushing myself to stay as close to 140 pounds as possible, and felt confident in almost everything I wore. I say *almost* everything, because short shorts were still somewhat of an issue. I wore them a few times running along the riverfront and they were more of a distraction than anything. I kept checking myself in every reflection to see how they looked. My thighs still didn't look like a typical runner's legs, and it bothered me.

In 2012, my husband and I went to Jamaica. I was in the best physical condition of my life and excited to wear a bathing suit in public. I bought a flattering black swimsuit that hid and highlighted everything it should. I also packed two pairs of short shorts in my suitcase. I was going to be in another country, and was determined to show off my new body with confidence.

I wore only my bathing suit in the pool and while tanning in a lounger on the deck. I wore the shorter shorts when we walked along the beachfront, and even allowed photos of me to be taken while I was wearing both. Sadly, I still wasn't as comfortable in my own skin as I was pretending to be.

I got a glimpse of my legs in the reflection of the mirrors that lined the elevator walls. It was a close-up image of the back of my thighs, and I could still see dimples. Despite how hard I'd worked and the fact that I was officially a marathon runner, my thighs were still quite flawed. They didn't look anything like the legs I envied in the runner magazines I was reading at that time. Even at my smallest, I was still focused on my flaws.

My new passion for fitness had inspired some pretty impressive physical achievements, and I loved every minute of it. Part of me wanted to keep upping the physical challenges, but it consumed too much of my life. I wasn't spending enough time with the people who mattered. I was missing out on a lot of fun and tasty food because I was determined to maintain my new body.

This is when I began to realize the importance of balance. I was already working on creating a better work/life balance; now it was time to develop a happier workout/social life balance. For those who've read *Dirty Secrets of the World's Worst Employee*, this is around the time I was working from home and had just lost my inspirational uncle to cancer.

Life felt fragile and I was driven to enjoy every moment to the fullest. That meant saying yes to dessert, sleeping in on the weekends, and spending my Saturdays eating and drinking with friends instead of running new personal record distances. I was worried about gaining the weight back again, but still able to manage my self-esteem using the "I'm not as heavy as I once was" perspective to reassure myself it was okay if I went one day without working out.

The Scale Is Shooting Up Again!

Over the next two years, I slowly packed on almost twenty pounds without really realizing it. I was averaging about five pounds every six months or so. It's a small enough amount that you don't notice it, and gradual enough that it didn't even occur to me that I was slowly transitioning from wearing size 6s into 8s and then eventually, most of what I was wearing was a size 10.

I saw the scale rising and allowed it to happen, because I didn't really want to maintain my strict workout and diet regime. I set myself an acceptable weight range instead of a specific target weight, so I had more flexibility. I figured anywhere between 140 to 155 pounds meant I was fit enough to feel and look good. I made myself a promise that I wouldn't stress over my weight as long as it wasn't inching up towards 160 pounds.

The biggest difference when I gained weight this time was my self-esteem. I was more confident than I had ever been, and rarely thought about the few extra pounds I gained. I didn't view my slightly curvier and flawed figure as being devastating or depressing as long as I stayed in the mid-150s.

I was still happy with how my body looked and willing to be brave in physical or social settings. I was still wearing more fitted clothing and bold colors. I kept myself in good enough condition that I could run, although I wasn't exactly running on a regular basis. I played floor hockey, walked the dogs daily, and enjoyed yoga and workouts with weights in my living room. My health was not suffering, but my stomach was definitely a little chubbier than it had been in years.

I thought I was finally comfortable in my skin, and no longer concerned that I didn't look like the flawless figures that you see on TV or magazine covers. I was content with myself and focused on new goals, liked becoming a successful author and advocate. I was purposely building new sensations of self-worth through positive achievements that went beyond my physical fitness. I wanted to feel good about myself as a capable woman and charitable human being.

Developing confidence based on who I really was as a person superseded my insecurities over my weight. I felt like I was finally loving my body despite its flaws when someone innocently pointed out my protruding belly and it didn't bother me the way it would have in the past.

Well, that's what I thought at first, but I wasn't quite there yet!

Up until recently, my reaction to intentional or unintentional jabs at my weight would normally result in either binge eating, drastic diets. or extreme workouts. When I was just starting to develop the concept for this story, my friend's young son asked me if there was a baby in my stomach while we were having appetizers and drinks on her back patio. I was sitting down and my round belly was noticeable through my clingy shirt.

There were four other women sitting around the table, and his mother gasped in horror. I made a joke about needing to diet and laughed it off. That's probably the reaction I would have had in the past, but this time, I didn't feel embarrassed or self-conscious.

My behavior didn't change. I continued to eat nachos and dip at the party and enjoyed myself without dwelling on the remark. I even jumped on her trampoline after the comment was made and didn't care when my shirt rose up to expose the very belly in question. The incident and meaningless comment from a small child wasn't immediately followed by a crash diet, excessive exercise, and regretful binge eating. I didn't for one second think that the other women at the table thought I looked pregnant.

The following day, I proudly ate Chinese leftovers for breakfast, a sausage for lunch and a taco salad for dinner. It was a Saturday, and I usually treat myself to less healthy options on the weekend. I weighed myself the following Sunday, saw 156 pounds, and smiled. My weight was fine, my belly was normal, and the silly comment didn't matter.

I joked about what had happened to a few friends who weren't there, jointed down a few points about the personal victory for this book, and didn't give it a second thought until I did my weekly weigh in the following Sunday. It wasn't the fact that a little boy mistook me for being pregnant that bothered me; it was that stupid number on the scale.

The needle bounced several lines over the 160-pound mark. My weight has always fluctuated dramatically from week to week, but this was a six- or seven-pound increase in seven days. It also meant I was now over twenty pounds heavier than I had been only three years prior, and the scale was moving in an upward trajectory.

I had spent the last two years relaxing for a few weeks at a time while I watched my weight rise up a few pounds, inching closer to 160, and then drastically increasing my workouts for a few weeks until I brought it back down to 150 pounds. This was the first time the needle was on the other side of 160 in about five years, and I started to freak out that the upward trend would continue. My weigh in that Sunday meant it was time to kick it up a notch before it got out-of-hand.

I was content with my weight if the first two digits were a one and a five, but the moment that five became a six, I panicked. I didn't want to pass the 160 mark, because I felt certain it would only be a matter of months before I rose above 170 pounds. In my mind, 200 pounds would be the inevitable conclusion if I didn't take action immediately. I could not allow myself to gain back all the excess fat that I'd worked so hard to burn off.

This was at the same time that I started writing this book, and a major influence on why I chose to write about body image and self-esteem. I was frustrated with how obsessive I'd become the moment the scale started to move in an upward direction. I'd instantly start exercising (sometimes I would do squats right there in the bathroom), and I'd immediately revert back to a stricter approach to my diet. I've been riding the weight roller-coaster my entire life, and I wanted to get off—permanently.

My self-control and discipline are fierce and able to keep me in check, but that mindset was hindering my freedom. I cared way too much about a few extra pounds, and for all the wrong reasons. The main thought that crossed my mind was disappointing anyone who had been inspired by my weight-loss journey, or anyone of my social media followers who admired my physical feats of strength. I was worried they'd think I was an unfit fraud.

Even my idea for the cover photo came with the knowledge I'd be shattering some delusions. There have been several different women who have gently pointed out that I'm in too good of shape to successfully carry out my mission. I couldn't be an advocate for loving your physical flaws, because my body was too close to the ideal size. I would joke that my clothes are deceiving while my internal voice was screaming, "Wait until they see how awful my legs actually look!"

It's embarrassing to admit I'm not as fit as I may appear. However, exposing years and years of obsessing like a psycho over something as vain as my weight sickens me much more. I'm tired of caring so much about carrying an extra ten pounds. Whether I weighed 150, 160, or even 170 pounds, I'm healthy and beautiful. The number on the scale is irrelevant, and I'm going to prove it.

Right?

I was finally starting to grasp this crucial life lesson and felt compelled to explore it in depth. I forced myself to really open my eyes and ears to the people around me. I focused mainly on average-looking women who either were very confident, or faked it better than I. I was trying to figure out what aspect of their appearance made them act as if they were so sure of themselves.

One of the best examples I found was the fifteen women I play floor hockey with every week. They range drastically in age and body size. Some are definitely in better shape than I, and others are noticeably heavier. All of these women are active, healthy, and truly beautiful. Regardless of their physical size, they challenge me every week we play. I've never thought that any of the women I played with needed to lose weight. I recognized that their bodies were healthy and acceptable, so why was I being so hard on myself?

I behaved like a hormone-driven man and dissected each one's physical appearance, so I could compare their imperfections with my own. I immediately noticed that I wasn't the only one with dimply thighs and a noticeable belly. I had been so focused on my own flaws that I didn't see the same in others.

I took a closer look at my friends and family, and it felt like I was seeing them for the first time. Several gorgeous, young women I know who regularly wear short shorts have cottage cheese thighs that look exactly like mine. They don't appear to have any issue flaunting their curves and sexy legs with bold pride. My admiration for these brave young women reconfirmed that I needed to put my own thighs on the book cover.

Up until recently, I never looked at other women with the same critical eye. I know women who judge everyone by their appearance, but I've never been able to do so. I was too busy being overly critical of myself to find imperfections in others. I only intentionally started forcing myself to dissect other women's physical appearance in an attempt to overcome my own self-obsessed body hatred. I made myself look at women whom I always viewed as being good-looking with the same intensity that I used to scrutinize myself.

To my surprise, they were just as physically flawed. I was so self-absorbed I didn't notice that almost everyone I met had some aspect of their appearance that didn't quite fit into society's expectations. At the same time, I finally realized that I wasn't as big as I thought. In fact, most of the women I knew were the same size or heavier. Some even admitted to weighing over 200 pounds, and I didn't think they looked fat. When I critically evaluate their bodies, I didn't see someone who had a problem with their weight. They didn't look obese or unhealthy. In my honest and judgmental opinion, these were attractive women with healthy bodies and voluptuous curves.

So why was I so disgusted with my own body?

Why does my self-esteem drop as the scale rises?

Why do I work so hard to hide my physical imperfections?

Why does it matter to me whether I weigh 160 or 170 pounds?

I didn't need to look perfect. No one else I knew did. Every body is flawed in some way or another, even the bodies we idolize on television or in magazines. Every person has an aspect of their body they wish they could change, but not everyone is as obsessed about hiding it as me.

I discovered a new (or possibly old and unnoticed) physical imperfection while writing this story. My boobs are not symmetrical. The nipples don't point in the same direction and one droops lower than the other. Recently, I've been inspecting my body more closely as part of my research, and the obvious differences in my breasts caught my attention in the mirror one night after my shower.

I usually avoid any long glances at my naked body, which is probably why I never noticed it prior to this. I have no idea how long they've actually been askew. My first reaction was shock and disbelief. Here I am, trying to love my chubby physique, and now my breasts are messed up. I wasn't sure if I was a freak, or if something was wrong with them health-wise.

Instead of hiding my imperfection, I told a few women I know about my discovery. They all laughed and assured me that most breasts are not symmetrical. Once I knew it was normal, all panic stopped. In fact, I thought my crooked boobs were quite appropriate. I already proudly show off my crooked tooth and crooked smile. It seems fitting that my breasts would be crooked too.

Although I will not show off my breasts in public (my husband might not appreciate that), I'm done trying to hide my physical imperfections. Everyone has something they don't like about their appearance. Instead of masking the things that make us unique, we need to learn how to embrace them.

I recently became addicted to Lena Dunham's awesome show, *Girls*. Her passion for writing and sincere comfort in her body was incredibly inspiring. She'd flaunt her pudgy belly in a crop-top with complete confidence, or spend the entire show exposing the majority of her chubby white body in a tiny green bikini. It was very apparent that she didn't have any issues showing off her bouncy butt or cottage cheese thighs.

My body looks a lot like hers, but I don't dare dress like her. I admire Lena Dunham's courage and think she looks absolutely beautiful, yet I struggle to dress in the same daring fashion unless I'm at my absolute fittest. I've spent too much of my precious time trying to find clothing that detracts attention from every soft inch of my physique. I'd rather be confident enough in my body to walk around in shorts and not care what anyone thinks about the dimples on my thighs. I'm getting there, but it's still a conscious choice I make daily.

Another reason I seem drawn to *Girls* is the show's ability to highlight the young women's poor choices with humor, rather than horror. Most television shows use people's mistakes as dramatic teachable moments that inevitably shame the person for their bad decision. No one is perfect; the characters on *Girls* celebrate their flaws, embrace their failures, and share their feelings honestly—even if it doesn't portray them in the best light. They are confident enough in themselves that they don't care how anyone else sees them.

While reflecting on my ongoing struggles with weight and self-esteem, I decided it was time to challenge my ability to be more like Lena Dunham. I wanted to prove to myself that I was finally done obsessing over it and ready to accept my body, flaws and all, even if I put on a few more pounds. I was already certain that my bright white legs were the only image that made sense on the cover, and I wanted to make sure my thighs looked as flawed and unappealing in the photo as they did in my head.

Yes, I sincerely want my raw chicken skin and unattractive divots immortalized in print. I could have gone in the opposite direction and worked my ass off (literally) to ensure my thighs looked good enough for the cover photo, but that wouldn't demonstrate that I finally love my body, flaws and all. That would just prove I could get back into great shape again. I already know I can lose weight any time I want simply by putting in the effort. The same is true for everyone reading this book.

I wanted to stop my current cycle of gaining and losing the same five to ten pounds every month and accept the outcome without it affecting my new self-confidence. The only way I could fathom achieving such a feat was to eliminate the scale, and forbid myself from doing anything associated with my weight-loss obsession.

Rules on the Road to Recovery

I haven't achieved much in my life without first laying down the rules of engagement. Setting tough goals and establishing a plan to reach them was the foundation I used to get my body into the best shape of my life and finish a marathon. I decided the same structure would be necessary to stabilize my self-confidence and accept my physical flaws. I came up with the following list of rules that I would hold myself to until I was ready to publish this book.

Rule 1—I am not allowed to diet or restrict my eating in any way.

I love food, and probably eat more than most women. It's one of the reasons I've never been super thin. Fortunately for me, most of the foods I love are somewhat healthy. I honestly enjoy veggies as a snack, and rarely crave sweets. To prove that my weight doesn't matter, I had to completely stop caring what I ate. Instead of debating every meal choice based on calories and fat, I would strictly base my decisions on what I felt like eating at the time. This was my favorite rule, and I was excited about embracing it enthusiastically!

Rule 2—I will not run any marathons.

I ended up running a second full marathon in 2012 with the hope of beating my original time, and only improved my time by two minutes. I am a marathon finisher, which is a major accomplishment on its own. I can accept that I don't have a strong chance of reaching the podium or ever finishing in the top one hundred, even if I became obsessed with training. I have nothing left to prove to myself, as far as running is concerned.

I finished my fifth half-marathon in October 2015, which was a few weeks before I created the rules for my road to recovery. I had already decided that would be my last long-distance running event, and I knew this guideline would be fairly easy to follow. My knees are not in the greatest condition because of all the running I've done, and the constant training consumes too much of my time. Plus, I ran my last half-marathon with my mom. It is a memory I'll treasure forever, and the perfect way to end that amazing chapter of my life.

Rule 3—I will not go to Ironcore Kettlebell Club.

It's my family's gym, the trainers are close friends, and I'm blessed with a free membership. I love it there, but it's not convenient with my work schedule. It's also a long way to travel, so it takes up my entire night and I can't walk the dogs with my husband.

The high-intensity workout is incredibly effective, but you have to do it at least three times a week to maintain it. Spending time with my husband, my dogs, my writing, and other social engagements are more important to me at this time in my life. I've accomplished enough physical goals for the time being. Now I want to focus on my mental and emotional needs.

Rule 4—I will not step on the scale.

I already cut myself back to only a weekly weigh in, but I knew this would be the hardest part of my plan. I figured it would be easy enough for me to still judge my body based on how my clothes fit, which gave me enough reassurance to put this rule in writing. Unfortunately, if my clothes started to feel tighter, I couldn't diet or workout at Ironcore to burn it off.

The only person who would hold me accountable for these four goals would be me. In the beginning of my journey, I relied on social media to force me to follow through on my commitments. I would post my intentions on Facebook, so my family and friends knew I was quitting smoking, training for a marathon, or trying to lose weight. I didn't want anyone to see me fail or give up (stubborn pride), so I had no choice but to finish what I set out to do. It's a highly effective method for reaching a goal that I recommend for anyone struggling to achieve something challenging.

I used that technique too many times, and I wanted to prove to myself that I could do it on my own. I needed to know if I could go months without obsessing over my body, and without leaning on others for support. I needed to know how I would react if I gained any weight.

Would I panic and start breaking the rules?

I added these rules to my plan when I was only about five thousand words into writing this story. It was the beginning of November, and my goal was to finish the book by the end of March. I was also working on my first fictional story at the same time, which realistically could delay finishing the book, pushing it more towards the beginning of summer.

Short season!

I knew my plan to enjoy life without obsessing over my weight would be much harder to follow through on if I couldn't hide any extra pounds under long pants and baggy sweaters. There wouldn't be much point in hiding my thighs anyway, now that I'm planning on promoting their dimply nature on the book cover. I was determined to prove that my weight struggles no longer ruled my life, and this felt like the only way I could retrain my brain not to base every decision on the weight-loss or weight-gain potential.

This rules weren't as easy to follow as I first thought. I almost broke my promise to myself the very first week, by stepping on the scale. I was feeling a little lighter than usual when I got out of bed on the first Sunday after establishing these rules. I love hopping on the scale when I think it's going to be a little lower than normal. It's a great way to start the day, provided your assumption is correct. There is no worse start to a day than feeling like you've lost a few pounds only to have the scale prove you wrong.

I pulled out the scale and was eagerly about to step on it when I remembered the commitment I had made to myself only a few days before. I stood there for a few minutes staring at it, debating whether or not to do it, before shoving it back in its hiding spot. A few days later I did the exact same thing when I woke up feeling heavy and bloated. I resisted the urge both times, but must admit I came very close to caving because I knew I could technically get away with it.

This level of self-control is relatively new to me, and it requires constant care and coaching. It started when I quit smoking six years ago, and has progressed into this unexplained ability to follow through on almost everything I set my mind to do. Run a marathon? Sure, if I say I can, then I will. Write a novel? Absolutely! Break up with the scale? Done!

I'm not Wonder Woman. There is nothing about my genetic makeup that grants me this power more than others. I'm just an ordinary woman who sets extraordinary goals, which means anyone else can do the same. I'm still fallible at times, and will change my mind about certain goals if success truly feels unattainable or not worth the effort.

For example, there was a time when I said I would finish a triathlon; I eventually gave up on that promise. I created a training plan, posted my intentions on Facebook, and was convinced I had what it took to finish one. Once I started training, I realized two serious flaws in my plan. I hated biking (it hurt my ass too much), and was not a strong swimmer. I went swimming a few times a week for several months before accepting the fact that this goal wasn't necessarily realistic or really necessary for my happiness.

My stepdad summed it up pretty well for me. If you're running and you get tired, you can walk. If you're biking and get tired, you can coast. If you're swimming and get tired, you drown. It sounds awful, but I was struggling to swim for two minutes without stopping after months of training. Drowning was an actual possibility, and not worth the risk just to feed my growing ego.

Achieving goals feels great, but it can also become an obsession. The natural high of accomplishing something challenging can become a dangerous drug, if you're not careful. In some cases, I've even done damage to my health and well-being because I was too determined to succeed. There were several times I pushed myself too hard during a run or workout and suffered from dehydration as a result. When I overheat, I get a pounding headache and usually end up vomiting. Too often, pushing myself to extremes resulted in being too sick to stand, too sore to move, or both.

It's important to reflect on what you're attempting and be honest with yourself about the reasons for wanting to achieve a specific goal. I had already proven my physical strength to myself when I finished my first marathon. I only wanted to finish a triathlon for bragging rights. In hindsight, that wasn't a good enough reason.

There was another valuable lesson I learned from training for the triathlon. As a non-athletic person, I hadn't spent much time in a women's locker room as an adult. I wasn't familiar with the carefree nature of how some women got in and out of their bathing suit. I was showing up wearing mine under my clothes, so I wouldn't have to get undressed in public. I drove home with a wet bathing suit under my yoga pants in freezing winter weather to avoid exposing my fairly fit body.

Most of the women, who I guessed were older than me, didn't have any issues exposing their flawed figures in front of each other. They lazily undressed and even held conversations completely naked, without hesitation. On the other hand, I immediately wrapped the towel around my waist the moment my pants came off. I didn't drop the towel until I was at the edge of the pool, and could quickly slide in the water without someone seeing my dimply thighs.

I was in the best physical condition of my life when I was training for the triathlon, and about twenty pounds less than I am now. There was no reason for me to hide any aspect of my body. Every woman in the changing room bravely exposed their cellulite and excess weight—except me. I recognized the difference between myself and these confident, carefree women, but I didn't think about the reasons behind it, at that time in my life. It wasn't until I gained the extra twenty pounds and started writing this story that I realized I needed to change the way I viewed my body.

Breaking up with the scale was an essential goal for my future happiness. It was an unhealthy obsession that controlled how I lived my life. I didn't realize how much that weekly reassurance meant to me until I forbid myself from stepping on it.

For the first month, I thought about pulling out the scale almost every time I undressed before getting in the shower. My stubbornness and my inability to lie to my friends (and anyone else kind enough to buy my books) forced me to not to break my promise. I'll admit that I still did some crazy sporadic workouts, took a laxative twice, and drank some wishful cups of green tea during the first month to fend off the potential weight gain, but I was at least successful at ignoring the scale.

Every so often I'd put on the cutoff jeans shorts I planned on wearing on the cover and pose, looking backwards in the mirror. It looked horribly disgusting within two feet of the mirror, dimply and unattractive within three feet, and somewhat acceptable around four feet away. My intention was to have the guts to take the photo from less than three feet away. I was sincerely worried that I wouldn't go through with it unless my thighs miraculously improved, which of course would defeat the purpose of my experiment.

Not knowing if I gained weight or how many pounds I may have put on was all I could think about for most of November, especially on days I felt bloated. I have a crazy Coke Zero addiction. I drink anywhere from three to five cans per day. I force myself to quit every so often, but it never lasts long. I pray that regular exercise and a relatively healthy diet will make up for my chemical romance. I'm punished for my choice quite often, and sadly, still haven't learned my lesson. Too much carbonation leads to a bloated belly, feeling fat, and constipation. That still hasn't convinced me to give it up, and I'm starting to wonder if there's actually cocaine in it. It's worse than a nicotine addiction.

I've quit enough bad habits in the last few years and wasn't ready to kick the can, literally, especially since it was a calorie-free filler that kept me from snacking. During the first month that I was following the rules, every bloated belly resulted in a good workout, green tea, and severe panic that the scale was on the rise.

Sometimes when I felt bloated, I would purposely drink a few beers or eat something unhealthy. I was intentionally forcing myself to love my body, even on the days I felt heavier. Enjoying something that I would normally limit was my way of proving that I didn't care if my belly was sticking out a little farther than normal. It always had to be a conscious decision to go against my gut instinct, and allow my stomach to expand even further.

My goal was to be happy as long as I was healthy, regardless of what number appeared when I finally stepped on the scale. I felt confident that my new routine of eating a mostly nutritious diet and regular exercise was keeping my insides in pretty good shape. There was no reason to get upset over a little bloating.

I'm curious to see where I'll be with my weight when I've finished my challenge. Fortunately for those who are reading this story, you won't have to wait months and months for the conclusion. For five months, I had to fight the urge to step on the scale on the days when my pants felt tight, and simply pray that I wasn't undoing all of my hard work. Any time that my jeans left a ring around my waistline, I'd start to worry about how close I was inching back up towards the 200-pound mark, for the third time as an adult.

Even though I wasn't running or doing intense boot camps, my body didn't appear to be changing. My clothes seemed to fit the same way, and I had the same energy level as I did prior to establishing the rules of engagement. I kept reminding myself that even though I couldn't see my weight on a scale, my body was relatively the same. It took about five to six weeks, but eventually I started thinking about it less frequently and began to truly enjoy my newfound freedom from the scale.

A major turning point was when I shared my new game plan with my closest girlfriends. I wasn't telling them so they would force me to follow through with my commitment to myself. I wanted their perspective on what I was attempting. I wanted to see if they had the same insecurities as I did, and how they would handle my new rules. The response was quite interesting.

My friends were all supportive of my efforts, but none of them were interested in following the same plan. In fact, the fittest of my friends, who is in better shape than I've ever been in my life, said she'd have the hardest time avoiding the scale. She currently checks it daily. She uses it as motivator to push herself harder.

I was shocked to see how quickly the subject matter resulted in my friends insulting themselves, while at the same time, complimenting each other. We've all had weight issues to varying degrees throughout our lives, and although we were four beautiful, talented, and confident women, the subject of weight instantly crashed all of our self-esteems. We spent the rest of the evening building each other back up.

Why is weight such a sensitive subject to the majority of women?

Anyone who watches television or reads magazines can easily answer that question. Women are displayed as flawless objectives primped and posed to evoke attraction and desire. Advertisements portray women as having perfect skin, silky hair, and unrealistic body proportions thanks to airbrushing and image-enhancing technology.

The reflections we see in our own mirrors fail miserably in comparison. We feel every roll of fat is evidence that we aren't meeting society's standards. The unrealistic expectations cause us to have an unhealthy obsession with our appearance.

There are probably a few days a week that I don't think about my body, but there are also several days when it is *all* I think about. Fortunately, I'm figuring out ways to avoid the triggers that push me to constantly assess and obsess over how I look.

It's ALL in the Jeans

During my experiment, I realized that it all boils down to how the jeans fit, which is trickier than usual for me right now. I own four pairs of jeans, and none of them fit me properly. I recently split the butt—that's usually the first place to burst on my pants—in my absolutely favorite pair. They were my confidence-boosting jeans, and I started wearing them twelve years ago when I first met my husband. Tossing them away was a major loss to my wardrobe.

I went out to buy a new pair and foolishly chose skinny jeans. I'm pear shaped; my waist is much smaller than my hips, butt, and thighs. I have lean and muscular calves, which look exceptionally tiny compared to my thighs. They didn't have a size 10 in stock, but they were a great bargain and the perfect shade of dark blue. I ended up getting the size 12 because it flattered my lower legs.

Unfortunately, the waist was way too wide, and they were droopy in the butt. My husband and a friend from work both pointed out that they were too big on me, so it wasn't just me being overly critical. It looked like I was wearing a baggy diaper underneath. I still wore them occasionally, but only with tighter tank tops that hugged the jeans to my body. I've never liked wearing belts because they added unnecessary bulk, so whatever I wore on top had to fulfill the role of a belt.

I still had three other pairs, but none fit like the ones that had just ripped. One was a size 8 that felt really tight, especially right out of the dryer. They made my butt look awesome, but my thighs looked thick. I bought them when I weighed around 145 pounds, so they didn't look nearly as good on me now that I was around fifteen pounds heavier.

I had two other pairs of jeans that were both a size 10. One fit a little too tight in the waist, and the other was a little loose in the waist. I'd wear the baggier pair when I felt bloated, and the tighter pair on days when I felt lighter. Neither of these gave me the same feeling as the pair that I threw out.

So I bought another pair of comfy yoga pants.

I already owned a few nice pairs, but I wanted something new in my wardrobe that fit comfortably. If the pants I wore to work felt tight by the end of the day, I'd just switch into pants with an elastic waistband when I got home.

I was determined to overcome my weight obsession. I needed to break the habit of basing my self-esteem and capabilities on the scale or how my jeans fit. In order to stop thinking about my weight, my clothes needed to fit comfortably. Jeans that cut into your waist or squash your thighs are effective fitness motivators, because they make you feel like you're bursting at the seams, literally! I've used that technique (wearing clothes that were too small) in the past to push myself to workout harder.

My goal was to feel better about my body, so I felt it was necessary to eliminate anything that forced me to assess whether or not I was gaining weight. I own several pairs of black workout pants and feel confident in all of them, even with my constant weight fluctuations. My success was dependent on creating that same feeling in everything I wore.

I still prefer to wear jeans at work or when I go out. Now I just make sure I choose which pair to wear based strictly on which pair fits best that day. For example, I'm usually bloated on Mondays from enjoying my weekend, so I wear the size 12 with a tight tank top covered by a loose sweater. That outfit fits me well, doesn't press into my skin, and flatters my figured. On the other hand, I exercise and eat well during the week, so I usually feel lighter by the end. If the size 8 jeans fit without digging into my gut, that pair can be the perfect confidence booster for a Friday night out.

Adjusting my wardrobe instead of my workouts and diet worked!

At first it was hard to avoid thinking about the scale, but the more I worked on this book, the less I cared about what it might say. If I lost weight, yahoo! That would be proof that you don't need to obsess over your weight to stay in shape. If I stayed the same weight, it would prove that I've found a good routine with my diet and exercise, and I no longer need to stress over it. I wouldn't be disappointed if I gained a little weight, either, since it would give me a better cover photo. I also feel certain that a few extra pounds won't interfere with my lifestyle or my happiness.

I no longer feel the need to give off the delusion of having a tight and toned body. There was an unflattering picture of me posted on Facebook the day I wrote this part of the story, and I had a noticeable belly roll in it. It was taken at a networking event that I was very proud of myself for attending. I'm still a little uncomfortable talking face to face with strangers about my books, and I faced that fear successfully. I saw a strong, confident, and happy woman when I looked at the picture. My eyes focused on my smile, not my stomach.

For the first time, I still saw an attractive photo despite the fact that I wasn't as thin as I'd like. I not only left myself tagged in it, I "liked" and commented on the photo, which I know will increase the number of people who see it. That soft tummy is the end product of eating and drinking with loved ones. I refuse to let an unflattering photo toy with my self-esteem, especially when I had just take a positive step in my career as an author.

I showed a friend that photo and I referred to it as the one where I looked fat but didn't care—once again labeling myself with the despicably inaccurate f-word. Her immediate response was that I didn't look big in the photo at all. She actually rolled her eyes at me in disapproval of my assessment. Upon closer inspection, I realized she was right. It showed a few folds in my sweater, which gave the impression of a couple small belly rolls. I didn't look overweight. This time, I was definitely being overly critical of myself.

The difference between now and how I would have handled that photo in the past is what actually matters. I didn't think it was a good photo, yet I didn't care who saw it. I accepted it and even pointed it out to others. I wasn't embarrassed that my stomach didn't appear flat and toned. I forgot to suck it in, because I was enjoying myself and no longer ashamed of how I looked.

I spent the last few years rebuilding my confidence, learning how to forgive myself, and be truly happy with the person I've become. I'm proud of my talents, kind heart, and voice as an advocate. Those are the traits that make me a beautiful person. Those are the reasons I need to love myself, no matter what the exterior package looks like.

Don't get me wrong, that doesn't mean I should stop taking care of my body. I believe in being physically fit and never want to lose my strength. I'm willing to let my thighs go soft for a more powerful cover shot, but I want to maintain a strong core and arms for my own well-being.

Muscles and stamina are both important for your health and longevity. That is why I still do a twenty- to thirty-minute workout with weights a few days a week, play floor hockey weekly, and walk with the dogs daily. The regular exercise and relatively healthy diet I've kept for the past few years seems to be holding my weight fairly steady, which means I have no excuse not to break free from my obsession with the scale.

I consider myself to be fit despite my physical flaws. I'm hoping to use this story to prove to other women that they can be in great physical shape and still have some excess fat. The textbook definition of fitness has nothing to do with a tiny waist, toned legs, and a flat stomach. Fitness is defined as the condition of being physically fit and healthy, or being suitable to fulfill a particular role or task.

It doesn't mention anything about weight or pant size.

I've discovered it is more effective and realistic to strive for good physical conditioning than it is for an ideal physique. It is nearly impossible for those of us who weren't blessed with a great metabolism and small frame to maintain a size 6 or smaller body, without it being the main focus of our daily lives.

My weight and pant size has been relatively consistent for well over a year because I put emphasis on being regularly active, I eat mostly good choices, and I spend time working on my arm and core strength. I can still physically do everything I enjoy doing. That's fitness. It has nothing to do with the current number on the scale, or the size of clothes you wear.

I started this challenge at the beginning of November, and had no idea what I weighed as I approached Christmas. The holidays always bring an abundance of temptations that I usually try my best to resist—or at least consume in moderation. Ever since I started running in 2009, I would lose five to ten pounds training for the marathon in October, and then not worry if I gained a few of those back over the holidays.

In 2014, I was dangerously close to 160 pounds even after training for my fourth half-marathon, so I did an extreme stair challenge during the daytime on Christmas Eve. I decided to do it so I could eat whatever I wanted without worry. I ended up being so sore from climbing stairs for an hour that I didn't really enjoy myself at any of the family functions. Sitting down hurt so much I wanted to cry, and I didn't have the energy to stand for very long. I ended up going home early on Christmas Eve and was in pain for the next three days.

This year (2015), I decided I would make the most of the holidays without giving my body a second thought. Although I hadn't been on a scale in seven weeks, I was pretty sure I was at the higher end of my preferred weight range, if not over. I knew the odds of gaining weight in December were pretty good; however, I wanted to prove to myself that it didn't matter if I put on a few extra pounds. Christmas is a time of eating good food with family and friends. I wouldn't be true to the purpose of this book if I wasted a minute of it worrying about calories or exercise.

I ate the chocolates and cookies people brought into work. I repeatedly filled my plate with deep-fried mushrooms and chicken wings at my floor hockey team's holiday get together. I even ate a massive donut at work one morning, knowing that my stomach doesn't handle sugar very well. I didn't want to rationalize turning down a tasty treat that everyone else was enjoying.

I was especially proud of myself on Christmas Eve. I filled my plate without considering calories and even posed for a photo that I knew would show off the weight I had gained. It was unseasonably warm and I was uncomfortably hot, so I took off my belly-hiding sweater. I was wearing a sleeveless, clingy shirt underneath that made my upper arms look quite plump. The shirt also seemed to accentuate the excess fat in my stomach, which is why I had chosen the sweater in the first place.

Despite my change in attire, I still encouraged my nephew to take a photo of me with my sister-in-law. My sister-in-law asked me to check the photo before she posted it to Facebook, and I only gave it a quick glance. I could tell it wasn't a flattering shot physically, and my smile was more awkward than normal, but I told her to post it without any hesitation. I knew it didn't make me look very attractive, and I was not being overly critical this time. However, I refused to let an unflattering image bother me for the second time in a matter of weeks.

My insecurities were no longer calling the shots!

My triumph continued throughout the holiday season. All of my favorite foods were on the table Christmas Day, and I didn't hesitate to eat exactly what I wanted. I loaded up on turkey, ham, stuffing, and scoop after scoop of my mom's cheesy cauliflower casserole. The holiday meal tasted far better than what I usually eat for dinner, so I ate as much of it as I could within reason. I eagerly took home some delicious leftovers as well.

I was wearing the size 10 jeans that are a little tight in the waist, and they started to cut into my gut by the end of the festivities. It was uncomfortable and would have been the catalyst to either binge eating or insane dieting if I hadn't already come up with a coping strategy. I changed into my comfy yoga pants the moment I got home, and didn't give my weight a second thought.

Well, I didn't give it another thought *that day*. It briefly crept into my mind the following day, when I was trying to decide what outfit to wear for my first radio interview. I knew I'd be on the air and my attire would only be seen by the host, but I still strategically chose a top that would cover my bloated Christmas belly.

Surprisingly, I wasn't frustrated with myself for having the excess pounds in my belly. I enjoyed gaining every one of them, and I was confident they would burn off naturally after the holidays when I returned to my normal diet and exercise routine. I may not have wanted to draw attention to it, but I was no longer allowing my weight to dictate my confidence.

I was even able to maintain my self-assurance when I busted the zipper on my jeans at work later that same week. For those who've read *Dirty Secrets of the World's Worst Employee*, I have a history of wardrobe malfunctions at work. I was wearing my tighter pair of size 10 jeans and one of the teeth broke off. I couldn't reconnect it and was holding my jeans up by just the button. Thankfully, I was wearing a long enough shirt that no one noticed my zipper wasn't done up.

I bravely took a long and critical look at myself in the mirror when I was trying to hook the zipper back on. My body wasn't perfect, but I didn't feel fat or ugly. I immediately saw the humor in the situation. My clothes have a history of falling apart in very public places, and it wasn't a reflection on my weight.

I could see that the waistline hadn't left a ring around my waist, which meant my jeans didn't bust because they no longer fit. I changed into my old yoga pants with the permanently-knotted tie when I got home, and I had no problem shimmying them up onto my hips. I double knotted the string when I was ten pounds lighter and couldn't get the knot untied. I figured as long as they slide on, I couldn't have gained much weight, if any. I took a realistic assessment of what happened and comforted myself before it had a chance to toy with my self-esteem.

There is no reason to be alarmed if a zipper busts or my shirt fits a little snugly. Even if I have gained weight, I know it's not the end of the world or a reflection on my worth. The only person who expects me to maintain this current frame is me, and I recognize now that the logic behind staying this size has been based on all the wrong reasons. I've been more concerned with looking a certain way than I have been about my health, and that's not healthy.

I've finally figured out that I'm not overweight now, and I've never been obese. I still hear lots of women who have fitter physiques than me call themselves fat, but now I realize that I used to be one of them. My perception of my body was delusional from years of obsessing over my weight. I saw myself as being significantly heavier than people who were almost the same size. I'm completely average, and there is nothing wrong with my body.

70

I'm more confident than ever, but I won't pretend for your sake that I'm cured. Insecure thoughts will occasionally creep into my head, but now I know how to immediately squash them. It's something I have to do consciously, but I don't need to rely on it as much as I did when I first quit the scale. It might sound a little odd, but I simply talk myself into loving my body. I use the same reasoning and reassurance method I mention at the beginning of this book—only now it actually works.

"It's just a little extra bloat. Your pants still fit. You've been eating well and walking the dogs daily. You'll just cut back on the late-night snacks for a bit, and do a little yoga before bed. It's nothing you need to worry about; you're still healthy. You're not fat, so don't even go there."

Sometimes I literally shake my head at myself when I'm done my little pep talk. Everything I'm telling myself is true, and the more I remind myself, the less often it becomes necessary to do so. On the other hand, I've tried to convince a few friends who are the same size or smaller than me that they are not fat, and it's like talking to a brick wall.

It gives me this overwhelming urge to shake them and scream, "WE'RE NOT FAT!"

I plan on insisting that a close friend reads this book as soon as I'm done, because it breaks my heart watching her ride the perfection roller-coaster week after week. She's absolutely stunning, and her body is the type most people envy. She's smaller than me and convinced she needs to lose twenty pounds. Several times a year, she busts her butt and gets down to that flawless figure she desires. She's in the cycle of burning it off only to let it gradually come back because she also likes to enjoy life's wonderful temptations.

During one of her workout and clean diet phases, she updated her status on Facebook saying she dreamed she ate some pizza! She was so relieved to wake up and discover it wasn't true, because she didn't want to spoil her weight-loss efforts. Although I encourage her commitment to getting into better shape, I wish she would realize that she's beautiful even with a few extra pounds. She pushes herself too hard; it's not something you can maintain unless it becomes your whole life. She's a mom of two boys and has an active social life. She has better things to do with her time than stress over a little extra weight.

Maintaining strictly muscles on bone is a full-time commitment, and an unrealistic expectation for most people. Unless your daily life keeps you active or you're born with a great metabolism, it is easy to put a few extra pounds of fat. That doesn't mean you're fat.

The word fat doesn't accurately characterize any human being, regardless of their physical size. Even if you have more body fat than muscle, you're not fat. You're a person, and the characteristics that define your worth can't be seen in a mirror or measured on a scale. In all honesty, I have no positive use for the word fat, and can't think of anyone who should be defined by such a demeaning term.

I'm even going to stop calling myself fat, which is a harder habit to break than you would imagine. I caught that evil word slipping out a lot when I first started writing this story. I was in a good place with my weight when I started writing it, despite being at the higher end of my ideal weight spectrum. Even though I didn't think I was fat at that time, I was constantly worried about becoming fat.

"I feel fat."

"This makes me look fat."

"I need to work out, I'm getting fat."

The word fat still sneaks out every so often, but I now catch myself and internally (externally if I'm around friends) scold my behavior. There is nothing wrong with my body. My thighs still have cottage cheese dimples, but I'm now excited that I'll be using an image of those dimples on the book cover, despite how they look. Yes, those are my legs on the cover.

I am so much more than just a chubby pair of legs!

I'm an author, an advocate, and a business professional. I'm a loving wife, daughter, and sister. I'm a good listener and a compassionate friend. My newfound confidence is based on the type of person I've become. It has nothing to do with losing or gaining weight. The first step in my mission is complete!

Dimply Leg Dilemma

Discovering confidence that came from something more stable than just my appearance changed my outlook on several different areas of my life. I stopped overthinking things, and decided to trust more in my gut instinct. I became less concerned with what other people thought of me, and as a result, I'm no longer a chronic people pleaser. I'm still helpful and humble, but I factor my own happiness into the equation when I'm deciding whether or not I can be of service to someone else.

The most surprising change was how I viewed my physical appearance. My looks have mattered less and less to me over the last few years, as far as hair, clothes, and makeup is concerned. I care about hygiene and wearing appropriate attire in certain situations. I enjoy dressing up for special events, but appreciate that I can wear comfy runners and jeans to work every day.

I've finally learned that I don't need to "get ready" every time I leave the house. I wear very little make-up normally, but would always brush my hair and touch-up my eyeliner before grocery shopping, walking, visiting a friend, the dog park, or even the gym.

I no longer bother putting on makeup if I'm going to be working out or running errands. I wear comfy pants when we walk with the dogs or go to the dog park. My husband puts no extra effort into his appearance before he goes out unless it is a special occasion. So, why should I?

I'm sure the single ladies will dispute my advice because there is always a chance of meeting Mr. Right when you're out in public. Good men, the kind that appreciate real women who have their own minds and shining personalities, usually prefer a more natural looking woman. They want to see your face how it will look when they wake up next to it.

I've worked around a lot of guys throughout my crazy career path and they usually talk freely as if I'm one of them. In all their dissecting and describing of women that they wish to be with, they never mention how nice her lipstick looks or the length of her lashes. Makeup might be worth the effort for a date, but men shouldn't expect you to look polished if they bump into you in a produce section at the local grocery store.

I think taking pride in your appearance is definitely important. However, you can't expect to look your best at all times or refuse to be seen when you don't. A few years ago, I felt like I couldn't leave my house without eyeliner and relatively controlled hair. Now, I can get up off the couch and head out the door without even checking in a mirror.

In the more recent years, the only aspect of my appearance I truly obsessed over was whether or not I looked fit. I worked so hard for three years to drop over fifty pounds and thoroughly transform my body. I wanted to keep that delusion, so I fussed over whether or not you could notice my new chub in whatever I was wearing.

I honestly don't care anymore what anyone else thinks of my body, mostly because I don't think anyone else actually thinks about my body. Well, besides my husband William—and I know why he's thinking about it. No one worthwhile in my life is going to stop loving me if I gain weight. Half of them are probably too worried about all the things they don't like about their own bodies to even notice what might be going on with mine.

Learning to love myself as a whole made me realize there's nothing wrong with my body. I'm probably the average weight for a 5'6" woman in her mid-thirties. There are countless gorgeous women all over the world who are the same size if not bigger than I am right now. Some of the world's sexiest celebrities, such as Jennifer Lopez, Beyoncé, Christina Aguilera, and Mindy Kaling, all have larger legs and voluptuous behinds, just like mine.

Why wasn't I able to see that my body ranked up there with some of the most sought-after celebrities in the world? I'm now comparing my body to the diverse figures that make up the majority of the world instead of an idealistic Barbie-doll frame that is a rarely mimicked by real women.

I've always thought Sara Rue was a great example of being stunning and sexy at any size. My deluded self-esteem convinced me I was quite a bit heavier than her, and not nearly as attractive. Now I think we've probably experienced the same weight fluctuations, and we're both fair-skinned beauties with bodacious booties. If I think her body looks great even at its heaviest, then I should think the same of mine.

Logic is the greatest defense against foolish insecurities.

Removing the "I hate my body" goggles and realizing that my legs are not nearly as disgusting as I thought created an unexpected dilemma. I was writing a book about loving your body, flaws and all, and now I'm no longer certain that I'm the best candidate for this crucial mission. Maybe the friends who tried to warn me in the beginning that my legs were not big enough were actually right. My weight struggles have been minor, compared to those of most people.

When I first came up with the idea for the book cover, I took a long look at myself in a full-length mirror, wearing my shortest pair of jean shorts. I was mortified when I turned to see my backside. My thighs looked awful, and I seriously doubted if I'd ever have the courage to pull off this plan. I considered secretly doing squats and yoga daily (something I do often anyways), so my family and friends wouldn't be embarrassed when I exposed such an unappealing side of my body.

I decided to try on the same pair of shorts after almost ninety days without the scale, dieting, or extreme exercise. I was feeling more confident than I had ever been, and wanted to test my self-esteem. I had to know if I would still feel good about myself when I saw the least appealing aspect of my body. I was sincerely scared to turn around, because I didn't know what to expect. Although I felt like I weighed about the same as when I laid down the rules in November, there was no weigh in to reassure me.

I was relieved that the front view didn't look that bad, so I spun around and braced myself for the worst. My reflection was definitely not the result I was expecting. My legs honestly looked normal. They were far from the images you see of sexy legs on TV or in magazines, but they were certainly not grotesque or embarrassing. A rational person would describe them as white, thick, and slightly dimpled. They didn't look like they could accurately be described as cottage cheese.

My thighs are normal as far as their appearance, and extraordinary in regards to the feats they have conquered. These large legs have carried me across countless finish lines and to personal victories, which were ultimately responsible for my greater self-esteem. I went from hating my legs to discovering sincere appreciation for their strength and power. Despite it being my intended outcome, I never could have predicted the influence this conclusion would have on my life.

Initially, the impact this level of self-assurance was having on my normal mindset baffled me. My goal was to write a book that would make me love my undesirable legs, so I could teach others how to love their bodies despite imperfections. Now that I love my body, my greater purpose that was supposed to come from reaching this goal felt like it was ruined. I want women to accept their bodies, regardless of size or shape. I was going to prove it was possible by embracing my chubby legs publicly.

How could I prove my point if my thighs weren't really that big compared to most?

Displaying my dimply legs in normal jean shorts on the cover no longer felt like it would be a bold display of bravery. There are countless women I know whose thighs look the exact same way, and they wear shorts that show off their upper thighs all summer long. I used to secretly wish I had the confidence to do the same, but I never thought those women looked disgusting or even unattractive.

Now I think our legs look the same.

Even though I hadn't stepped on a scale in months, I doubt my thighs have really changed that much. I've maintained the same wardrobe, eating habits, and exercise routines since long before I started this book. The year prior to writing this book, I watched the same five to ten pounds rise and fall on the scale every week. I'm pretty confident my body hasn't suddenly changed.

That sparked the most surprising string of thoughts to ever cross my mind.

Am I too fit to be effective?

Have I ever been as fat as I felt?

Could this story actually help women besides me?

I was worried women who are heavier than me would be insulted that I used to think I was fat. I remember how much it bothered me when my significantly skinnier mom would call herself overweight. It would always make me think *well if she's fat, then I must be obese.*

That's was the exact opposite of what I wanted to achieve.

My goal is to make all women love their bodies, not contribute to their insecurities. So please let me reiterate my initial discovery. Every body, regardless of size, should be loved and appreciated for its capabilities and contribution to your life. Your weight should only be a concern if it hinders your health or interferes with the life you want. If you're healthy, active, and able to do the things you want, then you've got a great body worthy of your love and attention.

I have a fantastic body; I just didn't realize it until recently. That doesn't exempt me from following through on the other goal I set for this story. I insist on proving to myself and my readers that I love this body even with its flaws, as minor as they may be. I'll intentionally create more flaws and even gain weight, if that's what it takes to drive this point home!

A cover shot of me wearing short shorts simply won't cut it anymore. Women far heavier than me do it quite often, so it's not really an act of bravery. As you discovered when you first saw the cover, I decided to up the ante. I went from a mortal fear of exposing my mid-thigh to anyone when this journey begun, to planning on showing *all* of my legs in tiny, bright pink underwear, with a tight tank top! My poor mother must be mortified!

Hopefully that still earns me the high-esteem compliment of being called brave.

I'd rather live up to my image of being confident and fearless than the illusion that I'm quite fit. My reputation should be based on my actions, not my appearance. That's what truly matters. That is also why I'm still going to love this body if I get on the scale and it shows that I now weigh over 170 pounds, which is a real possibility.

My pants are still fitting fine, but I've noticed my shirts are a bit more snug than usual. I may have gained weight during this experiment, and it doesn't bother me in the least. In fact, I wouldn't mind a few extra pounds, since I'm now certain my cover photo needs more dimples! I'm honestly allowing myself more treats than usual, and not pushing myself to work out very often. I can always rebuild my muscle afterwards, if I discover a loss in my physical strength.

My objective was a raw and honest image on the cover that demonstrated shocking bravery. Right now, my thighs only signify an insecure woman who took her minor imperfections far too seriously. I'm confident enough in myself now to let my legs get even softer, without fear of falling back into my self-obsessed battle with the scale.

I'll still be happy with who I am as a person regardless of what I weigh tomorrow, a year for now, or when I'm old and gray. The most crucial lesson in this whole story is that my self-esteem no longer fluctuates with my ever-changing weight. That rule should apply to every person reading this book.

There's nothing to gain if you let a few extra pounds hold you back from what you want in life. I used to dress in bland clothes and hide inside when I was heavier. Although I'm happy with my body, I am carrying a few more pounds than I would prefer. The difference is that I will no longer let that factor affect my bravery or how I live my life.

I was recently given an unexpected opportunity to test my new self-esteem in a very public way. The local TV station had a feature story on workplace bullying, and I had a chance to answer a few questions on camera about my second book. I had less than a day to prepare myself and my dress clothes were all a little too tight. I bought most of them three years ago, when I was still wearing size 6 pants.

When I first tried on potential shirts from my closet, everything looked fashionable—but clung to my new, rounder stomach. I'm sure it looked worse in my head, but I didn't want to be sucking in my gut for the camera when I should be focused on answering the reporter's questions.

Instead of stressing over which shirt looked best, I went shopping and bought a new shirt that hung loose around my waist. I choose a button-down dress shirt that had an eye-catching purple snakeskin pattern. It was definitely not dull or demure. My confidence radiated throughout the interview, because I felt good about myself and my body.

Self-esteem is 100 percent mental strength. It's controlled by our perception of our worthiness in the world. Learning to love all aspects of your being and winning that mental battle with insecurity is the key to having real self-confidence.

Confidence transforms your perception. When you're happy with yourself, you no longer feel the need to compare yourself to or compete with anyone else. You can appreciate their attributes and accomplishments without feeling inferior. I can look at my body in a mirror and feel good about it, because I'm not measuring it against some model's lean, air-brushed figure in a magazine.

I used to use the sight of my flawed figure as an exercise motivator; now I don't see my body as being flawed. There's an office building by my house that has mirrors instead of windows along one side. When I first started running. I'd check myself out in them when I ran or walked by, because seeing my big bouncy butt and the thickness of my thighs would motivate me to run faster and further.

On one of the first sunny days of spring, after four months without the scale, I took a break from writing to go for a brisk walk around my neighborhood. I passed the same building and took a peek at my reflection. This time, I loved what I saw. All I noticed was a strong and healthy woman, beaming with pride as she passed by.

I can be fit with flaws. My body is beautiful. I believe those sentences when I type them now. There's nothing wrong the thighs on the cover of this book, and I'm proud of myself for being to able to say it. My goal was to love my body, and I sincerely do.

I was discussing my mission with a supplier from my day job, and he brought up an excellent point that I must share. He's a good-looking guy, appears to be in relatively good shape, and has a stunning, exceptionally fit wife. He admits both he and his wife care too much about their weight, and have their own issues with the scale. It's always reassuring to hear that people who have enviable physiques have the same struggles as us average-looking people.

When we were talking about weight, I told him about my upcoming photo shoot in my leg-baring short shorts, and how I was petrified to take the photo at first. I told him that I now think my legs are average, I don't care about their flaws, and that I'm excited to share such a shocking image with everyone. His response made me pause, but only for a second. I was confident enough in myself not to question his sincerity.

"You know you're smaller than average?"

"Yes, that's true, but you never see legs like mine on the cover of a magazine."

"Yes, but you don't see people who look like magazine covers in real life."

He was absolutely right! The bodies we are trying to emulate are all airbrushed and Photoshopped to smooth out any imperfections. *Of course* my body doesn't look like theirs. That doesn't mean my body isn't in great shape. I've finally realized that I am in better shape than most women my age, and I should be grateful for this physique.

In the beginning of this story, I was constantly comparing my body with everyone else's, including celebrities and supermodels. I based my worthiness on what the scale said, and was under the impression that I weighed more than most. I pushed myself to achieve tough goals and maintain my figure in order to feel like my body was acceptable to society.

That mentality sounds so warped to me now. Of course my body is acceptable. It's strong, curvy, and unquestionably beautiful. My body doesn't need to be as fit as it was a few years ago, or look like the super-toned images that dominate mainstream media. I don't have that expectation of anyone else I know, so why would I put that kind of pressure on myself?

If you've ever seen photos of me with my friends and family, they're all absolutely beautiful. I've always thought every single woman in my life was attractive, for varying reasons. I used to compare myself to them, and I'd find several aspects of their appearance that I envied. Out of all the women who make up my life, there is only one who has a ridiculously toned, magazine-worthy body. I forgive her flawlessness because she's a fitness trainer. She uses her physical strength and lean physique to inspire women who want better health and self-confidence.

Besides the fact that most of the people I know are carrying at least a few extra pounds, there are no other obvious similarities in their appearance. They're not all blondes with blue eyes, big boobs, and long legs. Their physical features vary drastically. Just like the most sought-after superstars and models, the more unique and exotic they look, the stronger their beauty radiates.

Why can't we apply that same logic to our body size?

It's time to toss out the cookie-cutter fantasy type and stop forcing ourselves to strive for physical perfection. I know a lot of strong and healthy woman who are tired of feeling like they're not good enough just because they can't squeeze into a size 2, including me. Who decided that was how women are supposed to look? Men don't have the same high standards, so women shouldn't either!

Investigating Insecurities

Throughout this journey, I've tried to pinpoint what has made me hate my body in the past and why I'm able to love it now. The more I thought about the reasons behind my insecurities, the more I realized that my issues with my appearance had nothing to do with reality. I didn't feel fat because I was sluggish or unable to move my body with ease. I felt fat because I didn't fit the mold of what society has taught me a woman should look like.

The first and probably most influential factor in my body image was my mom. I do not blame her, since her own insecurities must have stemmed from somewhere or someone else, probably long before I was born. I'm also well past the age that I can blame any of my struggles on my parents. I've been making my own decision for at least the last twenty years, and need to take full ownership of this life.

My mom always insisted there was nothing wrong with my body. She never called me fat or encouraged me to diet. She did, however, refer to herself as being fat, and I've known since a young age that my mother was not happy with her thighs. I've been bigger than my mom in every aspect of my body since the age of twelve.

If my mom is fat, then I must be obese.

That was my old logic. I rejected my own body based on my mom's perception of hers. My mom's body was the first one I compared myself against, but definitely not the last. I was bigger than most of my high school friends, including the guys. Despite the fact that I was only a few pounds heavier, that small difference felt very significant when I was an insecure teenager.

The next factor was obviously my ex's verbal abuse and criticism of my body. I could write an entire story just on the damage he did to my self-esteem. Technically I did write one, since most of my first book dealt with Shane's verbal and physical abuse. It has taken over twelve years, but I can now say with confidence that I've permanently removed his voice from my head.

The most universal reason for my insecurities, my mom's insecurities, and those of the majority of the female population, is the mainstream media! Between showcasing fabulously fit bodies in most advertisements to the undeniable fact that most female celebrities are thin, it's pretty easy to assume that's how society expects our bodies to look.

Reinforcing insecurities is the key to increasing profits for countless industries. Corporations spend an insane amount of money on advertising to make us buy products we don't actually need. Their campaigns are designed to make us feel like we are inadequate or flawed, so they can sell us expensive solutions.

You can't sell cosmetics, gym memberships, liposuction, and dietary aids without first making the consumer feel like the product is necessary for their happiness. These products are not a requirement of our survival, and in most cases, they will not add any real value to our lives.

I studied marketing in college and many of my classes dealt with how to utilize ad copy and images to create an emotional reaction. The most effective way to make someone feel like they need to change their own body is by forcing them to compare themselves with happy, shiny people showing off their fat-free and flawless physiques.

The most obvious examples of this marketing tactic are the magazines you see in the checkout line at the grocery store. There always seems to be a collage of gorgeous women and muscular men with perfect bodies flaunting their skinny waists and oiled-up muscles over a variety of different magazine covers. All of these images are somewhat Photoshopped to create the illusion that the person on the cover is flawless.

Every year in January—my third month without the scale—these magazines are covered in catch phrases designed to inspire dieting. It's a new year, which means it's time to get that ideal physique before bathing suit season starts. You can shed those holiday pounds fast, if you buy our magazine and follow the diet secrets of your favorite celebrities!

"Get flat abs fast!"

"Bye-bye belly bulge!"

"Lose 20 pounds in just two weeks!"

"Celebrity secrets to getting a bikini body by summer!"

"Start the new year off right, and get the body you've always wanted!"

How does the magazine editor know that this isn't the body I've always wanted?

Almost every headline implies that there is something physically wrong with my body, and the magazine holds the answers to fixing it. A very small percentage of the world has the same toned physique as the person on the cover, and no one can Photoshop their reflection when they look in a full-length mirror. Almost everyone feels inferior to the unrealistic images on magazines, which fuels their insecurities.

Commercials for diet aides insult our intelligence with their absurd claims. They tout the potential for drastic transformation by promoting quick results with minimal effort. I'm especially insulted by the ones that promise you'll have a fabulously fit body without changing your diet or workouts.

"Simply pop this pill and the pounds will melt away."

How can that be a healthy solution?

Seeing all of these references to weight loss would normally motivate me to start dieting and exercising more frequently, but this year all I saw was clever marketing ploys. I actually believe that I have the body I've always wanted. It's healthy, and that is the only thing that truly matters. My attitude has changed, but I still have this overwhelming urge to change the culture that created my former perspective.

What would happen if we stopped buying into this notion that we should all have the same fatless, fit body?

There are countless major industries that would go out of business if people stopped striving for physical perfection. The weight-loss industry in the United States (sorry fellow Canadians, their stats are more impressive) is a 20-billion-dollar industry. Plastic surgery exceeds 12 billion annually, and reports show it has dramatically risen every year.

I doubt it would be possible to accurately estimate how much money the world spends on enhancing their appearance, but I'm willing to bet money it would be far greater than the amount we spend on our physical health. If we're being honest with ourselves, most diet or exercise related purchases are bought with the intention of dropping weight so we can look better; becoming healthier is just a happy side effect.

There are products created in the last century that wouldn't exist if we didn't care so much about our appearance. Take Spanx, for example! I believe in looking good and wearing clothes that fit, but I don't understand why we need to squish our body into life-sucking spandex just to smooth out our natural shape. Although I've always wished I could slip into something that instantly melted away the excess fat, I've never even tried on Spanx and have no desire to do so.

I'm constantly amazed by the products that are introduced strictly to feed on people's insecurities. My husband and I were watching *Shark Tank*, and saw the most perfect example of a needless product designed to fuel people's weight-loss obsessions. It was a dinner plate that calculates every calorie and gram of fat you're about to consume.

I'm not against calorie counting and watching your sugar intake, if your weight is a health concern. I definitely believe it's important to be conscious of what you put in your body. It's the obsession associated with such a product that bothers me.

The concept of weighing and analyzing every meal before you enjoy it is not healthy. If you need to monitor what you're eating, do it at the checkout line or in your kitchen before it's served. Quickly review your shopping cart or your dinner selection to see if most of what you're planning on eating comes from Mother Nature. Limit the processed foods, unnecessary fat, and products high in sugar when you purchase them, and you won't need some over-priced plate to do it for you.

My advice is to stop buying into all these crazy solutions and go back to the basics. The average person weighed significantly less a hundred years ago. Their diet consisted of what the earth supplied. Prepackaged meals, fast food, and chemical preservatives didn't really exist. Eating natural foods and being regularly active is the oldest and most effective weight-loss solution. Greedy entrepreneurs will claim to have created a better weight-loss method, but they are just temporary fixes that feed on our insecurities.

Weight loss is one of the most competitive and innovative industries in the world. It is also the most manipulative. Sales are completely driven by preying on those with low self-esteem. Their ads don't target people with actual health concerns who need to lose weight for legitimate reasons. The promotions are driven by catchphrases promising the body you've always wanted, or worse, a body that will drive the boys wild. The main focus of their pitch is on how their product will give you a thin, toned physique.

A person's physical size has no direct relation to their abilities. I've recently noticed several popular YouTube videos that showcase larger women practicing yoga. These women have the core strength to hold their entire bodies in complex positions, and they make it look easy. I watched one women hold a handstand perfectly still for at least 30 seconds. I've attempted the handstand myself, and can't hold it for more than a couple of seconds before I ungracefully topple over. Yet women who weigh significantly more than me can hold their heavier bodies for considerably longer. In my opinion, these women, whom society labels overweight, are clearly in better shape than I.

There are significantly skinnier people who are nowhere near as healthy as these 200-plus pound women. A new label (I hate labels) has surfaced, "skinny fat," and it's just as deadly as being obese. It refers to people who are physically thin, but lack adequate muscles or internal nutrition necessary for a truly healthy body.

Individuals who are skinny fat (every time I type that term I cringe, because it bothers me just as much as calling someone fat) assume their body's in great shape. They don't worry enough about their carbohydrates, sugar and sodium intake, or how often they exercise. As a result, many are high-risk candidates for diabetes, high blood pressure, or high cholesterol without knowing it. Quite often, the best looking exteriors are hiding the ugliest interiors.

It's proof that it's what's on the inside that counts.

A person's value in this world should be measured by how they treat people, the contribution they make to the world, and how they live their life. Their body should be judged on how well it functions, its physical capabilities, and internal health.

A person's weight or body shape should only be a serious concern if it's having a negative impact on their health, hindering their social life, or inhibiting their participation in fun, physical activities. If your weight is stopping you from enjoying the life you want, then yes, you should exercise more frequently and make better dietary choices. Work hard until you're healthy on the inside and then appreciate your body for becoming healthy, regardless of what it looks like on the outside.

If your body allows you do what you want without pain or struggle, then you should love it! That's all you should be asking of it. That's all most men ask of their bodies. Let's take male models and bodybuilders out of the equation. How many guys do you know who are obsessed with their weight? Maybe some who've been teased for being skinny or overweight as a kid, or suffer other significant issues with self-esteem, but the majority of adult men I know personally don't appear to care that much about their weight.

Some of them care more about their wife or girlfriend's weight than they do about their own, which is pretty inexcusable and should never be tolerated. I've heard obviously overweight men comment on their loved one needing to lose weight without even cluing in to the fact they need to do so as well.

Most men don't seem to think their bodies are unacceptable to society if they don't fit a certain mold. At least that was the impression I was under, so I decided to ask my husband how often he thinks about his excess weight (he has a bit of a belly) and his answer was simple.

"Only when it stops me from doing something I used to be able to do."

That's the right attitude! William was athletic when he was younger, and it bugs him now that he can't run as fast or throw as hard as he once could. If playing sports mattered to him more at this point in his life, then it would make sense for him to dedicate himself to getting into better shape. However, he is content playing floor hockey once a week, and walking the dogs with me.

To make sure William's opinion was the majority, I asked a few more guys I knew. Those who worked out regularly were more concerned with gaining muscle than their weight. Guys who were on the thinner side wished they could gain more weight. The guys on the heavier side said they would like to lose weight, but they didn't really think about it that often. I asked each man specifically how often they think about their weight, and the only one who didn't say "Rarely" said, "Only when I have to buy new pants because the old ones no longer fit."

I've observed that men who are overweight are quick to crack jokes about themselves. They eagerly point out their protruding stomachs and laugh at how much they are able to shovel in their months. I currently work with a guy who brags daily about how much eats for lunch. He's young and still has the metabolism that lets him eat like a pig, but it doesn't show on the scale.

One of his regular orders is a large gyro in a pita, Greek salad, and Greek poutine (fries covered with gyro meat, gravy, and feta cheese). Before I knew exactly how much food he usually orders for lunch, I made the mistake of asking him to order me the same thing as him. I ended up splitting it with another woman at work, and we still couldn't finish it all.

He is not the first guy I've met in my life who is proud of his excessive eating habits. I know both fit and flabby men who boast about consuming an entire pizza or finishing ten tacos after a night of drinking. How often do you hear a woman brag that she just polished off an entire box of cookies?

Most men are not controlled by the scale, although men usually are a major contributing factor for women's obsession with it. Men's insensitive comments and unrealistic expectations have a huge impact on a woman's self-esteem. The media floods men's mind with flawless women posing seductively to show off their perfect petite bodies. When you add in the incredibly phony representations of women in pornographic magazines and movies, it becomes the expectation of most men.

Men think that's what women should look like.

Women think that's what men expect.

In some cases, especially in certain cultures, other women reinforce this as the expectation. I work with several Asian women (Chinese, Vietnamese and Korean). All of these women are much smaller than me, yet several of them have told me their bodies are considered unacceptable in their culture.

A friend from China who couldn't weigh more than 130 pounds told me that in her culture, she was considered to be significantly overweight. Her mother was very concerned about her body, and specifically told her she needed to lose weight because she was too fat to find a man. Another Asian friend was living off of tea and broth for a few weeks because she was going home to see her family in Korea, and needed to drop ten pounds before leaving. She doesn't have an ounce of noticeable fat on her body.

From what these women have told me, that's the normal attitude of most Asian women and their mothers support this unrealistic expectation. None of the Korean, Chinese and Vietnamese coworkers whom I spoke with have mothers who approve of their North American bodies. They were constantly encouraged to maintain figures with virtually zero percent body fat by their strongest female role model.

Hearing my own mother refer to herself as fat when I was such a young girl had a negative effect on my body image. I couldn't imagine how psychologically damaging it would be to have my mother repeatedly tell me I needed to lose weight if I ever expected to get married.

I actually work with one Korean woman who I would estimate weighs less than 100 pounds. I'm honestly not exaggerating. She has a three-inch thigh gap, and her legs are skinnier than her knee caps. She wasn't married, and feared she never would be if she didn't stay that size. I can't understand how that's healthy or desirable. She looks fragile and ill, in my opinion.

Society's expectations of a woman vary all over the world. I did some research while writing this story, and was disgusted by what I discovered. Most cultures put more emphasis on a woman's body and sexuality than her mind and talents. We're objectified, broken down, and rated based on appearance.

How many times have you heard a guy rate a woman on a scale of one to ten?

Most guys don't hesitate to critique a woman's body and sex appeal. Some even have the audacity to say it in front of the woman, or *directly to her*, as if she was nothing more than an object to be either admired or rejected. A friend from work gave me a perfect example of this the other day.

She was approached by a male coworker, whom she considered nothing more than an acquaintance. The obviously overweight Middle-Eastern man was concerned about her, and felt the urge to share his opinion with my beautiful friend.

"You're gaining weight, and you need to do something before you get too big."

He commented that she had a pretty face, and the extra weight was taking away from her natural beauty. He told her that although he was allowed to gain extra weight, his wife had to stay under 130 pounds and so should she. If this wonderful woman wasn't already confident in her appearance, his inappropriate and inexcusable remarks could have severely damaged her self-esteem.

Although his behavior would be wrong regardless of her size, this coworker is relatively the same size as me. She's gorgeous, and already more concerned than necessary with the few extra pounds she's recently put on. The last thing she needed was some man she hardly knows telling her she needed to lose weight. Why on earth does a man think he has the right to tell a woman how she should look?

In some areas of the world, women are treated as sub-human. I've met some strong and determined Middle-Eastern women through social media, but based on everything else I've read, the women I've met are the exception to the rule. Most impoverished Middle-Eastern countries view women as property, and they're expected to be subservient. Gang rape and forced marriages are horrifically common, education and independence is discouraged, and domestic violence is tolerated and ignored.

I live in a country where that behavior is not acceptable and I don't have to walk the street in fear of being violently attacked, yet I willingly stayed in abusive relationship for several years, and slept with men because I felt obligated (albeit it wasn't as frequent or as violent). Even when I was in a healthy relationship, I felt the pressure to take care of all my husband and stepchildren's needs, ahead of my own. I thought it was my role to cook, clean, and serve everyone else.

I've changed my ways now, and if I hadn't, I never would have run a marathon or written a novel. Somewhere along my journey, I realized my needs and dreams matter, too. My husband started pitching in more with housework and my stepchildren grew up and became independent. I also set lower expectations for how my home needed to look.

Cleanliness in the kitchen and bathroom is a necessity, but I don't need to wash my floors every week. I have two massive dogs and a muddy backyard. Every time I wash the floors it takes me over an hour and they are dirty again within the hour. Why waste so much time chasing after impossible perfection? I'd rather spend my precious free time relaxing, working on my goals, or having fun with family and friends.

At first I felt guilty for putting my own needs first, but the benefits grow on you quickly. Caring for myself made me a happier person. Most of my close friends are moms, and they've all confessed to feeling guilty whenever they spend time or money on themselves. They think it is their duty to care for the family, and run themselves ragged trying to live up to the image of the perfect housewife and mother. So many women (probably many men, too) don't feel like they are doing enough for their loved ones.

In reality, they are doing more for the people around them then they are for their own happiness. As a result, they don't have the energy or motivation to keep it up. They end up falling short of their own high expectations, and feel worse about themselves. It's a self-destructive cycle you can break by identifying it.

The first step is easy. Stop expecting perfection. You will never have a spotless house, a flawless body, or a perfect life. Flaws are part of the fun, and life is so much more enjoyable if you live in the moment instead of worrying about living up to some delusional image. There is no need to keep up with the Joneses, or create the perfect life you pretend to have on Facebook. Chaos, clutter, and cellulite are the norm.

The second step is learning to love those very same flaws. Find ways to appreciate the things that make your life unique. Don't just accept the fact that you're not a perfect replica of the ideal woman (or man), embrace and love yourself for being different. I now love my crooked tooth, crooked smile, and even my crooked boobs because I guarantee those fabulous flaws are uniquely mine.

The third step will naturally occur once you stop putting pressure on yourself and accept that you can't look like a supermodel while being everything to everyone. You'll start loving yourself and doing things that make you happy. Once you are content with yourself, you'll end up being a better partner or parent by default.

It worked for me, and I think as a society we can tackle the unrealistic expectations we put on ourselves if we take it one at a time, starting with the size two waist and thigh gap model so many of us are striving to emulate. Not everyone can have a perfect body, regardless of how hard they work at it.

We need to change our perspective on weight and what defines an attractive body. All healthy bodies are beautiful. Carrying extra pounds isn't a sign we've failed at life. In most cases, it's a sign we are eating and resting, which are two necessities. If we can convince ourselves that our flawed bodies are attractive and lovable, maybe we'll stop chasing unattainable perfection in other aspects of our lives as well.

New Generation, New Expectations

Thanks to countless strong women speaking out against the unrealistic expectations, things are slowly starting to change. I see more and more commercials and campaigns promoting a broader spectrum of female body types. There are also some great brands that recognize the need for diversity, and are now basing their entire image on loving all body types.

Marketers are finally realizing that beauty comes in all shapes and sizes. Even *Sports Illustrated*, which has been a massive contributor to women's low self-esteem, is changing their ways. In February, 2016 they proudly promoted a sexy and vivacious size 14 cover model.

Seeing that undeniably attractive body in a bathing suit on the cover of a men's magazine means everything to me. The largest size I've ever worn is a size 14, and it's happened at the lowest points in my life. Those are the times when I hated my body and my self-esteem inevitably sank.

Ashley Graham looks amazing! I guarantee most heterosexual men are going gaga over her stunning body and sexy curves. How on earth did I think I was fat when I was her size? I am about two sizes smaller right now and up until recently, I was too embarrassed to wear shorts in public. This gorgeous woman has a comparable figure to the majority of women in the world, and she's wearing a swimsuit on the cover of the very magazine that usually makes the average woman feel unjustly inferior.

This larger-than-life example of a real woman's body makes the rest of us feel acceptable. I loved seeing how many women proudly shared the good news of Ashley's success on social media. It's a huge breakthrough for those of us who can't maintain that outdated and unrealistic size 2 waistline that we see on most magazine covers.

Who was it that decided you needed to have a specific body type to be considered attractive?

I was gravely disappointed, but not shocked, by the select few who criticized the photos, saying the image promotes an unhealthy body type. Ashley Graham is active, healthy, and looks toned despite her wider waistline. She's beautiful, and proof that stunning bodies come in all sizes. Negative attacks on her bold accomplishment are perfect examples of body shaming, and anyone who attacks her for her courage should be ashamed of their ignorance.

I was exceptionally impressed by how 5'11", 219-pound blogger Sara Petty responded to social media's judgmental attacks about what a 200-pound person should be allowed to wear. She combatted their unjustified opinions with undeniably sexy pictures of herself wearing a bikini, leggings, short shorts, and a crop top. The world jumped on board her campaign, and there was no denying that Sara Petty looked gorgeous in every photo she took. Her brave approach to the body-shaming critics and the overwhelming support she received is proof that the Instagram insults and Twitter trolls are now the minority.

Having a tight and toned body is an expectation that was drilled into our brains from a very young age. From our first Barbie Doll with the unrealistic waist and thin thighs, to the pop icons we worship as teenagers, and the celebrities who portray our favorite characters as young adults, you rarely see an average-size woman or someone with a chubby belly or thick thighs being idolized in the media. There was no one like Ashley Graham or Sara Petty when I was growing up.

The majority of the women I wanted to be like when I was a young, impressionable girl were a size 2, or 4 at the most. There were a few significantly overweight actresses, but they never played the role of a confident, successful woman. They were definitely not viewed as sex symbols.

Overweight female actors are usually cast as the comical sidekick or exceptionally kind friend who follows the extraordinarily beautiful lead actress around. Up until recently, television only showed larger women in secondary or subservient roles, which creates the perception that they are less important than their smaller counterparts.

In rare cases, the heavy woman is the lead character, like the classic show *Roseanne* or more recently, Melissa McCarthy on *Mike & Molly*. Unfortunately, on those shows there are constant jokes about their appearance and excess weight. There's always an equally overweight male by the woman's side, and a good portion of the storyline is based on the character's desire to lose weight. What could be a show geared towards shattering the negative stereotype society has of heavier people turns into a bodyshaming sitcom, reinforcing the prejudice that all overweight people are lazy and lack self-control.

How many times have you seen a slightly overweight, curvaceous woman like Ashley Graham as the leading female in a movie or television show?

I've even heard some celebrity interviews where overweight actors are told you can either be funny and fat or thin and taken seriously; there's no in between. Times are slowly changing and we are seeing more female characters with healthy curves and physical flaws, but it still appears to be the exception to Hollywood's normal standards.

Even in reality television shows that should represent the average person, there is an expectation for contestants to fit into the preferred body type, especially women. Do you remember the first few seasons of *American Idol* with Simon Cowell? He refused to vote for unattractive or overweight female contestants.

Simon insisted America didn't want a fat idol, yet noticeably overweight Ruben Studdard won in season two, when Simon was still a judge on the show. Apparently it's acceptable for a male singer to be judged strictly on his vocal abilities, but women have to look a certain way to be considered talented enough to win. Thankfully, there are new judges now and a broader range of female body types are being recognized for their beautiful voices. There are also shows like *The Voice* that hold blind auditions, so contestants are picked based strictly on the quality of their performance.

Slowly, but surely, society is changing.

Companies that used to be synonymous with body shaming and unrealistic expectations are finally seeing the benefits of diversifying their marketing strategies. Mattel has recently announced a new line of dolls that brilliantly flaunt a broader spectrum of body types. I've used the Barbie-doll reference throughout this novel because it's been an unattainable expectation that impressionable girls have strived to achieve for the last 56 years. Some women have even undergone extreme plastic surgery to create the same appearance as the unrealistic icon. I'm thrilled the next generation of young women will have more diverse toys to admire and emulate.

I hate to say anything negative about a woman I admire, but I was sad to see Oprah Winfrey in a weight-loss commercial this year. It's not something I would have thought necessary, unless she has health reasons behind her choices.

Oprah is one of the most beautiful, inspiring, and successful women in the world. The only bad photos I've seen of Oprah is when she had the big hair in the '80s, and that's just because I was a teenager in the '90s: we rebelled against hairspray and poufy bangs.

The commercial made it sound like she was bothered by her weight and she was fed up with how her body looks. Oprah should be so proud of all her other accomplishments that her weight shouldn't even be a consideration, provided she's physically healthy. I hope she's healthy, and that she learns to love her fabulous body.

By promoting icons with more obtainable bodies, showcasing natural beauty, and teaching everyone to love themselves for more than just their appearance, we can save our children from the same self-torture we endured. We need to consciously avoid contributing to their insecurities by making sure we're not degrading or dissecting our own bodies, or anyone else's.

I'm not naïve. I recognize changing society's emphasis on physical perfection is not as simple as it sounds. We can't control everything kids see and hear. Wonderful people can be bad influences without giving it a second thought. They don't realize the damage their comments may cause. Unfortunately, criticizing the human body is a normal and accepted part of our culture.

I was camping with my husband and his friends last summer, and a revolting conversation caught my attention. I was the only woman within earshot, and the guys were making fat jokes and rude comments about a couple of actresses who were slightly heavier than most celebrities. I won't reveal the celebrities' names since I don't want to contribute to their judgmental assessment.

What I found most interesting is that all four men had big round beer bellies, as well as gray or thinning hair. Two of these men were single and pretty unsuccessful in the dating world; the third was in a horrible relationship with a very heavy woman; and the fourth was my husband. I may not be thin, but I'm in much better shape than William (sorry, my love).

I didn't take their criticism personally, because I considered the source. I know that they were just being typical men and had no comprehension of how cruel they were being. None of them even considered that the actresses they were insulting were supermodels in comparison to their own physical flaws. I've known these guys for many years, and they put almost no effort into their own appearance.

What makes these men so critical of a complete stranger's excess weight?

If you pay attention to the people around you, this type of behavior is quite common. I've worked around men at various points throughout my career and have repeatedly overheard genuinely nice guys objectify women. I can admit I've even participated, although it's usually with subtle sarcasm. Every woman is broken down into random body parts while they assess how attractive she is in their eyes. In most cases, it's celebrities they don't even know personally, and they are basing their entire opinion of a person on how they look in a retouched photo.

That puts a lot of pressure on women who take them seriously.

I used to be one of those women, and only recently realized I don't care what any man thinks of this body. It works out well that my husband is attracted to my figure, but I wouldn't go back to being obsessed with my body if he wasn't. I didn't base my marriage on physical appearance, and wouldn't subject myself to being with someone who did.

Unfortunately, there are still a lot of women who feel like they are not good-looking enough or even acceptable in society if they do not mimic the slender body type that dominates their television and magazine covers. Women with fragile self-esteem think they've failed if there are any deviations between their natural beauty and the airbrushed images that men gush over.

Let's take a minute and think about why men gush over women with petite figures. Typically, men want a woman who is smaller than they are, so they feel more powerful and in control. Men prefer to be with someone they think they can dominate physically. It sounds almost like caveman mentality, and doesn't reflect our current expectation of gender equality.

Although I would hope that's not what most women are looking for in a man, it's something we sub-consciously select. Most women are compelled to keep their body and muscle mass lower, so it doesn't intimidate men. They tend to prefer tall or stocky men, and usually choose someone who weighs more than they do. I know I have chosen someone physically bigger in every one of my relationships. It's just another preconceived notion that perpetuates our obsession with the scale.

There are so many influences urging us to maintain perfect little bodies that escaping their grasp almost seems impossible. How can women filter the comments, sift through the stereotypes, and accept their bodies, flaws and all? I love my body now, but part of that comes from discovering it was fitter than I first thought. How can I convince women who are heavier than me to ignore all the demanding outside influences, and love their body at any size?

I sought feedback from a wide spectrum of women to see which brave and confident females were willing to follow my advice and break up with the scale. I spoke with women who were smaller than me, women who were the same size, and some that were heavier.

There were a few exceptions to every rule, but almost every one of the women who I feel certain have smaller or fitter physiques than I were obsessed with their weight and appearance. The women who were closest to the impossible Barbie-doll statuette were driven to extremes, because they were constantly chasing an impossible expectation. None of them felt they could forgo their ritual with the scale.

"I weigh myself every day."

"I won't let myself eat junk food or dessert."

"I need to work out daily if I'm ever going to get down to my ideal weight."

The majority of women who weigh around the same as me, which I think is most of the population, all felt much like I did when I started writing this book. They are not happy with their bodies any time they're carrying an extra five or ten pounds, and they spiral into extreme weight obsession if they put on more than twenty pounds.

"I'm too scared to get on a scale."

"I've cried looking at myself in the mirror."

"I start dieting any time the scale goes up a pound."

The biggest surprise was the women who I assume are a little heavier than me. Not one of these lovely ladies seemed really concerned about the scale or their exact weight. Most importantly, they all seem genuinely content with their lives, and confident in their appearance.

"I don't own a scale."

"I love my voluptuous curves and bodacious booty!"

"I've got more important things on my mind than weight."

I've known some of these women for a long time, and they don't seem to have any concerns when it comes to confidently wearing clingy or revealing clothing. They're healthy and active, but they're not trying to achieve or give off the illusion of having the typical bikini body. Gaining a pound here or there doesn't appear to have an impact on their self-esteem.

It shouldn't make a difference to anyone.

An interesting thought occurred to me when I was rereading and editing this story. I'm generalizing based on my own experiences and those of the women I interviewed, so it's more of a theory than anything based on hard facts. However, I've noticed a pattern of self-destruction whenever someone is chasing unattainable perfection.

Thin women are constantly exercising and watching what they eat, so they can maintain their ideal bodies. Average or slightly overweight women bounce back and forth with the scale and dieting, always trying desperately to lose a few more pounds. Slightly overweight people, who are more accepting of their bodies, don't stress over slight fluctuations. Those who are seriously overweight usually give up and stop caring what they've gained.

Could that be the mental battle that leads to obesity?

There is nothing physically unhealthy with being average or slightly overweight. However, society makes us feel like it's not good enough, so we begin a cycle of sporadic dieting, inconsistent workouts, and finally binge eating when we fail to achieve the results we desire.

Let's say you're a size 10 and you're always pushing yourself to become a size 4. You might get down to a size 6 or 8, but when it doesn't seem worth it because you still view yourself as being an overweight failure, you become frustrated and give up. You end up gaining back the weight, plus another ten or fifteen pounds because you use food to comfort yourself. Suddenly you're wearing a size 12 or 14, convinced you'll never obtain the size 4 body you idolize. At that point, it doesn't matter anymore; you might as well throw out the scale and eat whatever you want.

I've never been what I would now consider obese, but I remember how I felt when I was almost 200 pounds, before I developed hyperthyroidism. I didn't own a scale, ate crappy food without giving it a second thought, and spent most nights at home on the couch. Once I felt like I was too heavy to ever have an attractive body again, I gave up and let myself go...or grow, to be more accurate.

Most weight-loss plans involve some form of restrictive diet or time-consuming aerobics. You can maintain it for a while, but eventually you slip up and eat a cookie or skip your workout. You feel guilty at first, but then it happens again, because it is just too hard to maintain. Once you've broken your diet or workout routine multiple times, you chalk it up as another failed endeavor and revert back to your old ways.

Yo-yo dieting is hard on your metabolism, and actually causes your body to store fat. The more weight you gain, the less energy you have to work it off. We're essentially punishing our bodies for not being able to achieve unrealistic standards. Any commitment you make towards better health has to be something that fits within your lifestyle, and that you are able to maintain for the rest of your life.

Last year, when I realized I was hovering around the 160-pound mark on the scale, I caught myself falling into old habits of crash diets and guilt-fueled binge eating. If I saw the scale go up, I'd start working out excessively to bring it back down before it went past the "point of no return." I felt the pressure of the constant battle with the scale, and knew how easy it would be to give in and give up!

Instead, I decided to love my body and work towards keeping it healthy. I didn't get mad at myself or self-abusive. I chose to focus on my regular routine of daily moderate exercise and mostly clean eating. I didn't obsess over the number. Instead, I learned how to live without a number sign hanging over my head. I don't eat well and exercise so I can be a specific size; I do it so I can continue enjoying my active and healthy lifestyle.

While doing some research for this book, I discovered I'm slightly below the average weight compared to other women my height. I also found several "medical" charts that told me I'm overweight for my height. The only logical conclusion I could come to based on those two conflicting statements is that the majority of women are overweight.

Who are we overweight compared to, if we represent the average?

We're comparing ourselves to very trim physiques that are unrealistic for most people. When we look at BMI charts, fitness magazines, and most celebrities, we can't help but feel fat in comparison. The interesting thing is that we are comparing ourselves to elite standards, when we are regular people with hectic schedules and limited budgets.

Fitness professionals, models, and celebrities with toned bodies are paid well to keep it up. Most of the images we see are wealthy women with personal trainers, nutritionists, nannies, and housekeepers. These women have the time and resources to constantly work on staying in flawless condition. Then they are airbrushed and Photoshopped to look even more enviable.

Most people I know have full-time jobs, children, and houses to manage. Their lives are busy, and eating healthy doesn't always fit into their schedule. Sometimes they need to rely on processed food and quick snacks. They shouldn't feel like failures for not having the ability to maintain the same bodies as women who are paid well to look a certain way. They are not living the same lives as we are.

The more I write, the more I realize the dangers of comparing ourselves to anyone else. Everyone has different goals, commitments, challenges, and experiences. No two people are identical in any other aspect, so why do we think everyone should have the same body type?

Beauty comes in all shapes and sizes. It doesn't define our capabilities, nor should it control our self-esteem. We need to stop judging our bodies in terms of sizes and weight, and focus on their capabilities instead. Our confidence should stem from what we achieve and our impact on the world.

Fortunately, I've made significant progress in regards to that. I truly love myself. I'm proud of the person I've become, and can quickly talk myself out of any downward spiral of self-loathing and fat-shaming. I find myself caring less and less if other people are judging my appearance. In fact, I've stopped caring what people think of me in general.

I know I'm a good person, with good intentions and a kind heart. I believe other people see that in me, and I'm no longer affected by those who may not. I know my worth in this world. Learning to live your life without fear of judgment is the most freeing feeling possible. I wear what I want, I do what I want, and I say what I want because I know my intentions are always to help rather than harm. I put as much or as little effort into my appearance as I feel like each day, because looking a certain way is irrelevant to my purpose.

I live in the moment and make the most of every opportunity, because I'm not worried what others may think of what I'm attempting. I'm proud of what I do; I love myself, and that's enough. I don't need to censor or second-guess my behavior so others will like me. Writing this book has been instrumental in overcoming my insecurities and people-pleasing personality. I hope it does the same for those who read it.

We're more than just the number that appears when we step on the scale, and I'm not the slightest bit curious about what number is now. I'm not even sure what will make the best outcome for the story. Our weight and physical appearance don't really impact our contribution to society. The good I'm trying to do with my life is what I need to focus on, any time I get down on myself about a few extra pounds. The positive impact I have on other's lives matters more to me than whether or not that same person finds me physically attractive.

So why should I be obsessed with my weight?

Who actually cares what I weigh?

I'm tempted not to get on the scale ever again. It's been almost five months, and I've pretty much stopped thinking about my weight. If I didn't need to know my weight to conclude this story, I'm confident I would have been able to resist it for the rest of my life. I'm honestly not anxious or excited to step on the scale anymore.

I have a feeling it will be slightly higher, but that's been an intentional effort to gain weight for the cover photo. The closer I got to my scheduled photo shoot, the less I thought my legs looked flawed. I discovered the mirror in my bedroom amplified the appearance of cellulite and you could hardly see the dimples when I looked at them under brighter lighting. The three weeks prior to the photo, I stopped all leg exercises and ate more food than normal. Unfortunately, I caught the flu and probably lost a few pounds the week prior.

Despite being more confident than ever, I am a little nervous about how my thighs will look in the photo. I have high expectations of the impact they will have on women with similar insecurities. I know they are not as a bad as I originally thought, nor are they nice enough to be in a typical cover shot. I'm aiming for a delicate balance between being fit and flawed. I won't know if I achieved my goal until the book's released and I start receiving reactions from readers. That's a chance I'm willing to take.

I'm forcing myself to have faith that the photo will capture the flawed beauty I'm intending, and the scale will prove to be a nuisance that I never really needed to keep my weight under control. I didn't know if I could run a marathon before I crossed the finish line, but I didn't allow that uncertainty to stop me from crossing the starting line. Life is about taking chances. If my image and this story makes one insecure person love and accept themselves, flaws and all, then it's a success.

I'm already a success and that means my experiment was as well. I went from being embarrassed by every extra pound to being proud of every imperfection. I've reached a level of confidence where I know I'm just as smart, good-looking, and talented as everyone else. High or low, I'm no longer obsessed with trying to perfect this body. Regardless of the results, it's already the perfect body for me.

Does what I weigh really matter?

It doesn't to me anymore, but I think those who have followed this story thus far are going to want a conclusion to my little experiment. You've listen to me rant about my weight struggles for way too many pages now not to find out where I ended up on the scale. I feel certain that I'll love every inch of this body, regardless of what number appears.

I decided to make my weigh-in date the first of April, which would be five months from the last time I got on a scale, and two weeks after the cover photo shoot. I was bouncing just above 160 pounds at the beginning, and am expecting I won't be too far from my starting weight. Before I stepped on the scale, I made a promise to myself that I would not allow the results to change how I felt about myself. It took me too long to feel comfortable in my skin, and I refuse to go back to the way I used to be.

In actuality, I weighed 165 pounds.

This will be my last time on the scale. Initially, I felt a little disappointment over the fact the number had slightly increased. There was a part of me that was hoping my weight would have gone down, but I knew it was unlikely since I spent the last month neglecting my usual healthy routine.

I gave myself a little pep talk and reminded myself that the cover photos I took prove there's nothing wrong with my body. It only took me a few minutes to shake off the results, and I'm honestly thrilled at the thought of living the rest of my life without the weigh in. Life without the scale has been liberating, and I have no desire to return to my obsessive ways.

My friend took the cover photo two weeks before my weigh in, so I couldn't say for sure if the woman on the cover weighs 160, 165, or 170 pounds. My weight has fluctuated that drastically within a couple of weeks (sometimes days) in the past, so I may have weighed anywhere in that range. However, I do know that the woman on the cover is a strong, confident, liberated woman, who felt completely comfortable dancing around in that incredibly revealing outfit while her friends instructed her to move around in a variety of poses and positions (thank you Louise and Kim). She didn't crack or even cringe as she opened and sorted through 150 photos emphasizing her modest cellulite and food-belly bump.

I actually loved the photos and felt they captured what I intended, even though my legs didn't have enough dimples to be classified as cottage cheese. I went through each image and only deleted a few because I wasn't smiling or looking into the camera. I didn't delete any because I didn't like how my thighs looked. I picked out the top thirty shots that demonstrated the following necessities: a big smile, my tattoo, and noticeable dimples on my thigh. I left the final decision of which image to use to my talented friend who designed the cover, so that it would be based on creativity rather than vanity.

I'll confess I almost reverted back to my old ways when I received the cover proofs from my talented friend. Although I thoroughly examined the photos a month prior and felt confident my legs were better than I ever imagined, my heart raced with fear at the thought of using this flawed image in every social media post to promote the book. I immediately focused on the size of my shapely ass and crooked smile since there wasn't enough cellulite on my thighs to stress over.

My friend sent me half-a-dozen different designs and I originally picked the image where I looked my best. My legs looked smooth, my ass looked *Kardashian* and I had a sexy smirk that I loved. I knew it wasn't flawed enough, yet I didn't feel brave enough to choose one with multiple issues. Then I gave my head a shake. What would be the point of this book if I didn't choose a cover with a little cellulite showing, a nice love handle sticking out and an overly-eager, cheesy smile?

I'm not cured of the self-conscious thoughts that creep into my head, but I can talk myself through it and rationalize my insecurities. I have every right to be proud of this body and I embrace every flaw in my perfect book cover image.

My cover photo is measured in bravery, not pounds.

Maintaining this Frame

I couldn't write a book about loving your body without advice on how to create a body that's a little easier to love. I'm not referring to fit, tight, and toned bodies like we see in the magazines. You've just read pages and pages about why the actual size and shape doesn't matter. I have no intention of undoing everything I've hopefully taught you through my experiences. Your body is beautiful, regardless of its imperfections.

There's not one particular body size or type that is easier to love than another. A lovable body is one that doesn't cause pain or discomfort throughout the course of everyday life. I want to help everyone achieve a strong, healthy body that is capable of anything, regardless of its measurements.

Achieving an ideal body has nothing to do with how much you weigh or what size you wear. Focus on improving your physical capabilities, ease of movement, and overall health. The goal is to live a long and active life in which you're not stressing over fluctuations on the scale. So, start the process by tossing out your scale. I'm proof that you don't need to know your weight to have a body you love. In fact, stepping on the scale causes more self-esteem issues, heartaches, and weight gain than life without it!

Instead, measure your success on what you can physically do. Try holding a plank for 30 seconds, press a twenty-pound kettlebell over your head, or walk for a mile. Do it again the next day, but try increasing what you did the day before by 5 percent. When you consistently perform exercises that test your strength and endurance, you will inevitably improve your fitness level and physique. If you can gradually accomplish greater physical feats each day, you'll become stronger because of it—that's an undeniable reason for you to love your body.

Unlike cardio exercise, which requires you to sustain it until your heart rate reaches a certain peak, strength exercises have an almost instant effect, especially if they're performed on a repetitive or daily basis. You can lift weights, hold challenging yoga poses, or perform bodyweight-driven exercises for short periods of time and still strengthen your muscles.

Prior to intentionally slacking so my thighs would look more flawed in the cover photo, I would exercise for about five minutes a few times throughout the day. I know every fitness trainer is either shaking their head furiously or resisting the urge to toss this book in the garbage right now, but I swear it works. I do twenty squats, then hold a squat for twenty seconds. I follow it with twenty standing, high-knee to elbows (each side), twenty calf raises, twenty arm circles in each direction while holding my calf raise, and then a one-minute plank. It's fast, easy and effective!

These exercises are not designed to burn calories or help you lose weight quickly, because that's not what's important. They are geared towards strengthening muscles, building endurance, improving balance, and boosting your energy level. I work in an office, where I sit at a computer nine hours a day. Taking a five-minute break to perform this simple routine helps my circulation, heart health, and mental exhaustion. I don't do it to lose weight, I do it for my overall well-being.

Another necessity to creating or maintaining a lovable body is proper nutrition. If you make sure you're fueling your body with mostly nutritious foods, you'll have more energy to be active and will feel better in general.

There's no denying that eating crappy food will make you feel sluggish. Every time I eat a donut or something sweet, especially early in the morning, I feel gross and unmotivated for hours. There are still times I can't resist the temptation, but I make sure to balance it with vegetables and protein so I don't crash as hard once the sugar rush fades.

I always try to practice the 80/20 principle when it comes to healthy eating. About 80 percent of the food I consume would be considered health-conscious choices and the other 20 percent are the rewards I give myself to fend off any cravings. If you repeatedly deprive yourself of your favorite snack foods, you're more likely to binge or overeat the first time you cave in to the temptation. In the same respect that you need a good work/life balance to be happy, you need to balance good food and tasty temptations to stay healthy.

Another tip I've found that helps maintain my physical conditioning is eating more frequently. I try to eat a handful or two of something every two to three hours. The grumbling in my belly lets me (and anyone around me) know if I go longer than three hours without eating. Eating smaller portions more often will boost your metabolism and fend off binge eating.

I actually have a reputation at my current job for always eating, and there's a recurring joke that I work for food. I'm not embarrassed (although I would have been a few years ago), and even contribute to that image. I love food and will eat almost anything. That's why I've never been successful with restrictive diets. It's also hard for me to turn down free food, which happens to be available quite often where I work, so I limit my portion size and try to choose the healthier leftovers more often than not.

I balance eating relatively well with regular activity. You can't lie on the couch day after day and expect to love your body. It's not giving you anything to love. My healthy body has allowed me to join in on countless fun activities. I can go downtown dancing with my friends and last for hours without feeling any urge to sit down, with or without the assistance of Red Bull and vodka.

Two of my closest friends have trampolines, and bouncing on them for ten minutes seems to turn back the clock, mentally and physically. Sometimes we jump on it with their kids, and other times, it's just the adults. We've had a blast working our legs and core muscles without ever considering that we're actually exercising.

I'm proud of my body because it has pushed past pain and accomplished incredible feats like climbing a twenty-foot wall with a rope, and jumping over a pit of fire at my first Warrior Dash. It was a truly awesome event to participate in, and I only got to experience it because my body was strong enough.

I have a humiliating story from the Warrior Dash that clearly demonstrates how perverse and self-conscious my mindset was prior to writing this story. I set a personal goal to complete every obstacle, regardless of how tough or dirty, and was exceptionally proud that I stuck to it because things were more physically exhausting or disgustingly muddy than I had envisioned.

At the very end of the race there was a 30-foot-high slide that propelled you deep into muddy water. When I was at the top of the slide, I noticed a man with a professional camera perched at the bottom. He was taking pictures of everyone. As much as I cringe at unflattering photos, I beam over ones that make me look fit or fabulous. I wanted a picture of me racing down the slide with my arms in the air and a huge smile on my face. Unfortunately, I didn't anticipate how fast I would fly down the slippery slide. Within seconds, I was submerged in a cesspool of swampy bacteria. My mouth was open and my nose was unplugged, so plenty of filthy fun found its way through my body.

I never saw the photo I desired, but my foolish vanity didn't go unpunished. I was sick for the next two weeks with a sinus infection that turned into a throat infection. I also developed a permanent pearl-sized lump in my neck, which was later diagnosed as harmless foreign debris after having an ultrasound. My doctor checks it regularly, but removing it would be considered cosmetic surgery since it's not having a negative effect on my health. Although I think it's gross and wish it wasn't there, it acts as a reminder of how my thinking has changed.

I'll participate in similar challenges, but next time I'll wear the rubber nose-plugs and clench my mouth tight. I sincerely wouldn't care if there's photographic evidence of my goofy getup. Discovering the consequences of my vanity sparked a major realization for me. Prior to writing this story, I was more worried about my how I might look in a photo than the amazing goal I was in the process of accomplishing. As a result, my physical health and appearance suffered.

I wasn't being active and adventurous for the right reasons, and it backfired. Exercise should be a fun and freeing part of your life, driven by the desire to improve your health and happiness. It's a blessing, not a burden.

There are so many simple ways you can incorporate some form of physical activity into daily life. I walk with my dogs for thirty to sixty minutes every day, I play floor hockey once a week, and try to squeeze in my little five-minute workout a couple times per day, especially during the work-week. I also try to fit in a twenty- to thirty-minute workout once or twice on the weekend to test my current fitness level. I've combined all the exercises that make me feel strong—yoga, planks, squats, and presses—and created an enjoyable at-home workout that is designed to develop muscles, build core strength, and improve my balance.

If those things don't fit your lifestyle, find something that does. It could be playing tag or a sport with your kids once a week. Maybe you prefer to go swimming, biking, or horseback riding. To those who clean their own houses, vacuuming, sweeping, and any other form of housework that involves challenging your muscles or vigorous physical movement is considered being active. To those with young children, chasing and carrying them around is definitely an effective workout.

You don't need to join a gym or hire a personal trainer to maintain a healthy level of fitness. Those are great resources if you're currently lacking muscles and need to improve your health, but if your workout plan is too time-consuming or physically draining, you won't be able to keep it up for the rest of your life. A workout should never feel like something you have to do. It should just be a part of your life that you enjoy, or plan on doing anyway.

When I felt sluggish after slacking on my leg exercises for the photo shoot, I decided to build back some strength with some much-needed spring cleaning. I swept and mopped three flights of stairs followed by painting two flights (two coats per flight). The next day I beat a few rugs on the clothes line and scrubbed my entire stove, as well as my usual weekend bathroom cleaning, dusting, and laundry. Instead of running or a workout,

I spent a couple hours each day catching up on my chores after going for a long walk each morning with William and our two energetic labs.

The following weekend, I attended a hot yoga class a friend was teaching with my two fiercely fit friends. We sweated our butts off during the class and then went out for a nice healthy dinner afterwards. I drank a considerable number of beers and mowed down a massive plate of nachos later in the evening, but didn't feel guilty since I already made a few healthy choices earlier in the day.

For me, this was a fun day with wonderful women I love being around. Attending the yoga class had nothing to do with wanting to lose weight; otherwise I could have resisted ordering nachos. It was the same weekend I weighed myself for the first time in five months and finished writing this story. I intentionally ate and drank what I wanted to prove to myself that even though I gained a few pounds, it hadn't changed the way I was enjoying my life.

I watched my moderately flawed body in the mirrored walls during the yoga class and didn't care. I struggled to hold a few of the positions, but wasn't embarrassed. I was happy with what I could do, and appreciated the opportunity to participate in something healthy with my friends. I felt a sense of relief and accomplishment, because my insecurities were having no affect on my behavior or self-esteem.

There's no required workout or established rules regarding how to stay fit and health. Any combination of healthy food choices and various forms of physical activity can create a body that's easy to love, regardless of its dimensions or gravitational pull towards the earth. You'll love it because of everything it allows you to do. Just remember, don't do it with the intent of watching the scale drop (hopefully you'll follow my advice and throw it away before you even start). Do it with the goal of improving your health, mobility, and stamina.

Any goal you set for yourself should always be driven by what you'll gain from achieving it. Weight-loss commercials and fitness professionals always seem to focus on what you'll lose. They promote their products and workouts by boasting about how many pounds will melt away, the dress sizes you'll drop, and how many inches on your body you'll end up losing if you use their revolutionary system.

Instead of worrying about shedding pounds, focus on what you'll gain from your efforts instead of what you'll lose. Think about the energy, flexibility, and physical strength you'll have if you eat better and increase your level of physical activity. Just imagine all the new goals you can set for yourself, if your body has the physical conditioning to perform at its best.

Every person has their own ambitions in life, and there's no right or wrong way to live your life. If you're motivated to work out daily and compete in tough sports or physical challenges, then go for it! If you just need enough energy to care for your kids and household without collapsing from exhaustion, then make that your objective. It's your body, your life, and your agenda.

Everyone knows that our bodies need nourishment, exercise, and rest to function properly. What most forget is that our bodies also need a little pampering. It's crucial that we reward our bodies for all the hard work we put them through. I understand how hard it is to find any free time in your chaotic schedule, but it's crucial that you set aside at least an hour a week (or thirty minutes twice a week) to spoil yourself.

I started taking long, candlelit bubble baths once a week. I pour myself a tall glass of Guinness, turn on the tunes, and soak until I'm a wrinkled prune. Many of the ideas for this story occurred to me during my luxurious escape. I never used to think I had the time, or that it was worth the trouble, but I'm obviously comfortable admitting when I'm wrong. That thirty-minute break from daily responsibilities is now a treasured part of my weekly routine. It keeps me happy, and that's always worth the time.

If you're going to obsess over achieving anything in your life, make it happiness. Feeling good about yourself, your body, your choices... it all has a cyclical effect that will improve your life and those around you. The happier you are, the better you treat people, and that fantastic feeling spreads like wildfire.

Could you imagine what the world would be like if everyone was happy, confident, and secure in themselves?

Of course, tragedies and heartbreak would still happen, but we would learn how to lean on each other instead of hiding our problems out of fear of judgment. As a society, we'd become a better support system. We can actually improve the world simply by loving our flaws, admitting our mistakes, and treating others with the same compassion we expect in return.

I'm often asked how hard it was to be brutally honest about the mistakes I've made. In retrospect, it wasn't hard at all. I know the damage it causes when you keep it to yourself, and I know the healing that happens when you talk about it openly. Discussing any aspect of my flaws and failures actually feels empowering now. The same can be said about admitting or exposing our physical imperfections.

Yes, I've gained a few pounds, and it wouldn't hurt me to lose a few pounds. It also wouldn't hurt me if I put on a few more. The best part of this entire book is that I won't be stepping on a scale again to find out. Dissecting the reasons for my previous body hatred uncovered a body that I now love unconditionally. Out of gratitude for my strong and sexy physique, I'll do my best to keep it healthy.

That's all that should matter when it comes to your body. Stop stressing over insignificant physical imperfections, and choose to love your body for all it does for you. Embrace your flaws and let them empower you. Regardless of your body's current shape or strength, your physical appearance has very little to do with who you are as a person. Build your self-esteem from within, do the things that make you happy, and take care of your needs. That's the secret to being happy. Love yourself unconditionally and create a life that's easy to love.

Writing this story gave me more confidence than I imagined, and I pray reading it does the same for you. I'm proud to see my cottage cheese thighs on the cover, because I know they no longer control my self-esteem. I think they look awesome, and I'm brave enough to compliment myself publicly. I've worked hard to create the life I wanted, and I'm proud of the woman I've become. For the first time in my life, I love all aspects of my being. I hope the same is true for you.

Never forget to love yourself, flaws and all.

More Than Just the Space I Fill

By Jenn Sadai

I am more than just the space I fill.
I'm a person, with purpose and strong will.
My value is not measured by the size I wear.
I demonstrate my worth with the love I share.

I try to make the most out of the space I fill.
I'm a thinker and a dreamer with poetic skill.
My impact goes beyond the shape you see.
I benefit this world just by being me.

I'm someone with feelings, not someone to feel.
I'm the minds I change and the hearts I heal.
I am not defined by my reflection in a mirror.
I will not hide body parts out of shame or fear.

I'm a leader and a fighter with a powerful voice.
This is my life, my body, and my choice.
I am far more than just the space I fill.
I'm an author, and advocate spreading good will.

Afterword

For those who may be wondering if I've broken my rules to recovery since writing this book, I'm proud to announce the answer is no. When I stepped on the scale April 1, after five months without it, I was genuinely indifferent about the results. It's now two months later and I have no idea what I weigh nor do I care. I still eat healthy most of the time, but I never turn down a beer or feel guilty if I eat something that I once considered a no-no.

I went from being obsessed with my weight to only weighing myself once in the last seven months. Even when I gave myself that goal, I wasn't certain that I'd be able to follow through and truly break the habit. Every time I worked on this story, I was reminded of the toxic effect the scale had on my life and became more determined to permanently sever the relationship. Our breakup is official and I know better than to repeat my past mistakes.

The scale no longer defines my worth.

My value is immeasurable.

Sincerely,

Jenn Sadai

About the Author

Jenn Sadai's goal as an author is to use her talents and life experiences to inspire anyone struggling through similar challenges. Her first book, *Dark Confessions of an Extraordinary, Ordinary Woman*, was released in February of 2014 and delves into the dark consequences of domestic violence, drug use and depression. The personal side of Jenn's story is a raw and honest account of how her life came crumbling down and the journey she took to put the pieces back together.

Her second book, *Dirty Secrets of the World's Worst Employee*, follows Jenn's crooked career path and the obstacles she faced before discovering her true calling. Her professional journey addresses critical issues such as gender equality, sexual harassment and workplace bullying. *Cottage Cheese Thighs* is Jenn's third book in her self-proclaimed "Self-esteem Series." It tackles the sensitive relationship between our weight and the way we view ourselves.

Jenn Sadai is a proud Canadian, born in Windsor, Ontario, where she resides with her heroic husband, fantastic stepchildren, and two lovable labs. She lives life in the moment and is always willing to try something new. You can reach Jenn through the various social media links on her website, www.jennsadai.com.

Coming Soon

Jenn Sadai plans on publishing her first fictional story, *Her Own Hero*, in 2017. She recently started writing her fifth book as well, *Choosing to be Childless*. This self-help memoir will focus on teaching the world that a woman doesn't need to become a mother to have a fulfilling life.

www.ingramcontent.com/pod-product-compliance
Lightning Source LLC
Chambersburg PA
CBHW032008040426
42448CB00006B/529